"Helen Wood, researcher, writer, teacher and feminist, shows how media meaning making has been studied. Read Audience to get an excellent overview or to find out where we need to take audience research next!"

Joke Hermes, *Professor of Practice-based Research in Media, Culture and Citizenship at Inholland University*

AUDIENCE

This accessible guide through audience studies' histories outlines a contemporary Cultural Studies approach to audiences for the digital age.

This book is *not* a survey of all existing audience research. Instead, its chapters survey parts of the field in order to draw some 'through-lines' from older traditions to contemporary debates, giving students a 'way in' to thinking about the current landscape from an 'audience-sensitive' perspective. In order to do this, the book utilises a series of verbs to organise and cut a path through audience research and register its ongoing relevance today. These verbs are: audience, anchor, mean, feel and work. The list is not exhaustive and the reader is invited to think about what verbs they would add or change throughout the book. *Audience* suggests renewing the importance of 'form' as a cultural process and in 'circling-back' to Cultural Studies' 'circuit of culture', it proposes a modified framework for 'the digital circuit'. Each chapter opens with a particular scenario for the reader to reflect upon and asks a specific question to help orient the account of research that is to come, especially for those new to Media and Cultural Studies and to audience studies.

Written in an engaging and accessible style, this book is ideal for both students and researchers of Media and Cultural Studies.

Helen Wood is Professor of Media and Cultural Studies at the University of Aston, Birmingham, UK. She has published widely on gender, television, class and audiences, including the books *Talking with Television* (2009) and with Beverley Skeggs *Reacting to Reality Television* (2012). She was formerly a long-serving editor of the *European Journal of Cultural Studies*.

KEY IDEAS IN MEDIA AND CULTURAL STUDIES

The *Key Ideas in Media and Cultural Studies* series covers the main concepts, issues, debates and controversies in contemporary media and cultural studies. Titles in the series constitute authoritative, original essays rather than literary surveys, but are also written explicitly to support undergraduate teaching. The series provides students and teachers with lively and original treatments of key topics in the field.

Cultural Policy
David Bell and Kate Oakley

Reality TV
Annette Hill

Culture
Ben Highmore

Representation
Jenny Kidd

Celebrity
Sean Redmond

Global Cultural Economy
Christiaan De Beukelaer and Kim-Marie Spence

Marxism
Karl Marx's Fifteen Key Concepts for Cultural and Communication Studies
Christian Fuchs

Deep Mediatization
Andreas Hepp

Information
Micky Lee

Media Engagement
Peter Dahlgren and Annette Hill

Audience
Helen Wood

For more information about this series, please visit: https://www.routledge.com/ Key-Ideas-in-Media--Cultural-Studies/book-series/KEYIDEA

AUDIENCE

Helen Wood

LONDON AND NEW YORK

Designed cover image: Getty Images

First published 2024
by Routledge
4 Park Square, Milton Park, Abingdon, Oxon OX14 4RN

and by Routledge
605 Third Avenue, New York, NY 10158

Routledge is an imprint of the Taylor & Francis Group, an informa business

© 2024 Helen Wood

The right of Helen Wood to be identified as author of this work has been asserted in accordance with sections 77 and 78 of the Copyright, Designs and Patents Act 1988.

All rights reserved. No part of this book may be reprinted or reproduced or utilised in any form or by any electronic, mechanical, or other means, now known or hereafter invented, including photocopying and recording, or in any information storage or retrieval system, without permission in writing from the publishers.

Trademark notice: Product or corporate names may be trademarks or registered trademarks, and are used only for identification and explanation without intent to infringe.

British Library Cataloguing-in-Publication Data
A catalogue record for this book is available from the British Library

ISBN: 978-1-032-53975-1 (hbk)
ISBN: 978-1-032-53974-4 (pbk)
ISBN: 978-1-003-41457-5 (ebk)

DOI: 10.4324/9781003414575

Typeset in Times New Roman
by codeMantra

Contents

	Acknowledgements	viii
	Introduction	1
1	**Audience**	9
2	**Anchor**	30
3	**Mean**	56
4	**Feel**	84
5	**Work**	118
6	**The Digital Circuit**	140
	Index	165

Acknowledgements

To my family and friends who have lived with that 'book', the four letter word that they cannot mention, for far too long – thank you. You believed that one day I would settle down to write it when I did not. It has been a difficult on-and-off process – too much to take on, too much to think about, too much change and too much pressure to speak across Cultural Studies itself.

Thanks to my editor Natalie Foster for limitless patience and still wanting the book despite everything.

My huge thanks to students at the University of Leicester and the University of Lancaster with whom I have talked about media, audiences and Cultural Studies. I have tried my hardest to be clear thanks to you. To my brilliant colleagues at both institutions for the comradery and conviviality that is so cruelly being pressed out of academia: Jilly Kay, Melanie Kennedy, Natasha Whiteman, Kaitlynn Mendes, Alison Harvey, Jack Newsinger, Mark Banks, Beverley Skeggs, Tracey Jensen, Imogen Tyler, Laura Clancy, Michaela Benson Eva Li, Siarong Fong, Maarten Michielse, Allison Hui, Debra Ferreday, Graeme Gilloch, Ann Cronin, Patricia Prieto-Blanco.

Thanks to Annette Hill, Peter Lunt and Joke Hermes for inviting me to a seminar in Lund in May 2023, which gave me the energy to get back to completing the book and the confidence to tell my own version of audience studies.

For reading some of the chapters and giving me some insight into their much more brilliant brains, I am ever grateful to Laura Clancy, Joke Hermes, Jo Littler, Bev Skeggs, and Heather Savigny. To Jilly Kay for being the best critical friend, reader and pal – now you teach me – I cannot thank you enough. To Karen Boyle for staying with me from the beginning of our academic careers and for being smart and full of joy and rage in equal measure. The limitations are of course my own.

To my co-editors of the *European Journal of Cultural Studies* who live the critical project of expanding the field with such care and commitment: Joke Hermes, Anamik Saha, Jilly Kay, Jo Littler, Yui Fai Chow, Jess Martin and Annelot Prins – thank you for all the conversations about what Cultural Studies is and should be. Many, many thanks Joke for encouraging me to carry on – with some Dutch love and analytical precision. A big thank you to Ann Gray with whom I started my academic journey as an undergraduate at the University of Birmingham and found my academic home. Thank you Joke and Ann for welcoming me into the European Journal of Cultural Studies, where I am so proud to have contributed. You have both been a huge inspiration and support ever since.

To the brilliant Helen Wheatley who has put a smile on my face during the most turbulent of times – team Helen forever!

And, finally, thanks to Max and Hannah, for putting up with me and bringing total joy …most of the time!

INTRODUCTION

Media relationships with audiences are complex, multi-layered and almost impossible to produce any overarching truths about. In Ofcom's (the UK communications' regulator) 2022 survey[1] into British lives online, they describe a picture that we might well expect: online shopping and dating continues to rise; children are circumventing parental controls and surveillance; and they are privatising their TikTok accounts and maintaining 'finstas' (Fake Instagram accounts). But, their research also shows a set of shifting sands which might pull in different directions against any stable predictions about what our continued media lives are coming to mean. For instance, three quarters of children who are gaming do so socially with someone else – a practice which rose significantly during the Covid pandemic during periods of isolation – which challenges common-sense understandings of a lone isolated gamer-identity. At the same time, the research shows that on social media young people are scrolling more rather than sharing, because they are seeing less content from their friends as platforms have become dominated by professional content from brands, celebrities and influencers. Social media is in fact becoming less *social*. Any framework for media audience studies therefore has to be flexible enough to cope with continually shifting

DOI: 10.4324/9781003414575-1

INTRODUCTION

and evolving techno-social arrangements, at the same time that it must hold onto a sense of 'conjunctural' critique. By which I mean a commitment to understanding the precise configuration of the social, cultural, political, technological and economic arrangements in any particular moment and any in given place in time. Whilst the answers may not be stable, we must continue to ask questions of what media relationships with audiences *mean*, even when the answers are highly contingent and contextually dependent.

This book has been challenging to write because of the seismic changes in the media landscape, which have rendered any understanding of what 'the audience' is more fragile and potentially even more inaccessible. Where then to even start? Given that so much has changed through the internet, social media and platformisation, that we may want to think of ourselves more as users, consumers, content generators or even by subjectivities generated by the apps themselves, (TikTokers, Instagrammars, Snappers) at the same time as we are still surely readers, television viewers and cinema-goers. Audiences are also increasingly transnational, pointing us to questions which must take on board their global scale. (Athique, 2016) In these contexts, far beyond what Nicholas Abercrombie and Brian Longhurst (1998) referred to as an emerging picture of 'dispersed audiences', do we even need to think of audiences at all? It might be tempting to cast audience research as belonging to the now outpaced broadcast era. The challenges of the digital media landscape can seem to overshadow previous work conducted with so-called 'legacy' media, implying that we must start again in order to capture an environment that is now characterised by: convergent media; participatory culture; user generated content, produsage, data surveillance, algorithmic prediction and so on. Yet amid the pressure to capture technological change, we must still put the experiential and the social at the heart of a Media and Cultural Studies approach because we cannot afford to be bedazzled by the capacities of the highly mediatised landscape. We need to be able to interrogate media relationships with people in order to grasp their imbrication with the big social and cultural questions of our time – widening social inequality, faltering democracy, new gender orders, racial capitalism, the environmental crisis and other intersecting dimensions of crises. This book suggests that a Cultural Studies' approach to audiences is still the best place to start.

INTRODUCTION 3

The book highlights some ongoing questions about the cultural and social for any further attempt to study audiences, arguing that we should distinguish between the need to understand media and social change, as separate to how the field of audience research has developed. No simple task. The point here is that it is not only that transformations in the media environment have driven, and should in some ways continue to drive, the evolutions in our field, but that we also need to understand *how* and *why* the questions of media and society have been asked in a particular way at any given time. These are two separate evolutionary narratives that do not necessarily run in parallel – audience research does not just develop in harmony with technological change. My contention here is that if we insist upon seeing these narratives as neatly in tandem, then we are in danger of leaving behind observations made about audience engagements with older technologies, and leaving behind important insights into social and cultural relations that have continued relevance to our field.

The main driver of this book therefore is to insist that whilst it is important to understand newer ways of thinking about media and audiences, we should not only be guided by changes in media and technological architectures, but we also need to be driven by the important and continuing political questions of the social order. Media studies has become a massively expanding field of inquiry, but we might still need to 'circle-back' for analytical tools through its intellectual histories and through the histories of media, from time to time. It is simply not enough for media analysis to be *only* occupied by technological change and, guided by Raymond Williams (2003), it never has been.

The study of audiences has always been difficult because to do so has always been part of wider concerns about 'society' and 'culture'. Since Ien Ang's (1991) important work, it has long been understood that 'audiences' often come into being when people are looking to describe them, usually for their own political ends. That very simple fact remains stable even in a context where the apparent distinctions between media and society are almost too blurred to define. The overriding feeling that it is difficult to discern what, in modern mediated industrialised societies, exists outside of media does not and should not usurp our concern for what this means for the uneven structuring of

4 INTRODUCTION

the social and the role of culture in the maintenance of the status quo. In fact, it becomes imperative that we begin to decide how different media, and not a reified idea of 'the media', are responsible for a range of activities which both create, as well as sometimes attempt to undo, the asymmetrical relations that are part of deeply mediatised societies. By reifying ideas of 'the media' we might fall into a trap of not being specific enough about the differentiated forms of power that they enact and the elite cultures that they serve since particular concentrations of symbolic resources in institutional centres continue to be legitimated even in a more dispersed media landscape. These are important questions to which media audience research should be focussed, placing lived experience at the centre of the debate.

This book therefore is *not* a survey of all existing audience research – especially as it may be derived from many alternative disciplinary fields including psychology and marketing. Rather it makes the case for contemporary media studies to recognise the achievements of Cultural Studies' audience research and acknowledge their continued salience for the contemporary hyper-complex digital environment. Its' chapters survey parts of the field in order try and draw some 'through-lines' from older traditions, to contemporary debates, in an attempt to give students a 'way in' to thinking through the current landscape from an 'audience-sensitive' perspective. The book does not get too held up on labels for the audiences – whether they are users, or readers and so on unless it is helpful to explain a perspective. 'Audience' to my mind, as a verb, offers a perspective that makes those distinctions less pivotal. The book does survey a good deal of audience research, but there is a folder as big as the bigger than the book itself on my computer called 'sections from the book' where I have been forced to crop and tailor a specific account from my own perspective for a book of this size. This is therefore a perspective driven by Cultural Studies with its disciplinary promiscuity and with a particular way of seeing and doing things. As the technological explosion and expansion of digital architectures and data extraction throws up new challenges, it seems more imperative than ever that, following Ann Gray 'we must continue to make sense of the ways in which culture is produced in and through everyday living, what Raymond Williams called "lived cultures" (Gray, 2003: 11). Remember, we still live everyday lives, however spectacularly they are shaped by media transformations.

INTRODUCTION 5

There will be, no doubt, for many scholars in the field, important absences and some developments given short-shift, but the selection process involved the practice of 'joining up the dots' through 'classic' audience research to where we are now. In order to do this, the book thinks about a series of verbs that cut a path through audience research to register its ongoing relevance. These verbs are: audience, anchor, mean, feel and work. But it is also quite clear that there are verbs that could have just have easily been written like 'play' with a greater focus on relationships with gaming and fans fan studies or perhaps 'educate' 'learn' with a great focus on citizenship and democracy. So these chapters do not in any way delimit any perimeters for audience research, they represent my own selection which has informed my own research and the reader should see the book through that lens from the start outset.

Throughout the book, you might want to think about what verbs would you add or change. In fact, this book constantly asks something of you, the reader, throughout these chapters. Each chapter opens with a particular scenario for you to reflect on as you read and asks a specific question to help orient the account of research that is to come, especially if you are new to Media and Cultural Studies and to audience studies. The final chapter asks you to think of your own scenario – quite literally to do the work and to conjure an 'audience-sensitive' perspective perhaps before embarking upon an audience research project. This is because the underlying project of the book is to encourage students to carry out more audience research with a Cultural Studies' approach in order to understand the complex ways in which we live with and by digital architectures that generate these ever-complex textual, social and technological arrangements.

Chapter 1: 'Audience' asks the question, 'Where is the audience here and now?' This chapter opens with the scenario of the cult of Peloton fitness bike and sets the scene for the varying aspects of media complexity that the audience researcher now needs to take into account, and invites the reader to position an understanding of audience within them. Many of these accounts, which theorise our densely mediated societies from a kind of grand-narrative perspective, have taken place without researching the experiences of audiences. I then set out the key framework for the book which, drawing on John Fiske (1992), centrally takes 'audience' as a verb, rather than 'audience' as an object – drawing on important legacies in Cultural Studies' audience research and

6 INTRODUCTION

pointing towards their re-casting for the digital age. It sets out Cultural Studies' particular framework of 'conjunctural' analysis as a plea to become 'radically contextual' and committed to a critical project.

Chapter 2: 'Anchor' asks the question, 'How can audience histories, help us to understand social change?' This chapter opens with the scenario of 'Housewife aged 18' from my archival research and uses anchor as a verb and as a plea to the student and new audience researcher to always historicise. It draws on some of the legacies of audience research to make a case for the contemporary researcher to employ a keen sense of the histories of audiences in order to be aware of how they are heart of changes in social and cultural relations. It is important to understand that these histories are not geographically even and that we must pay attention to the normalising tendencies of media histories of the west. This chapter suggests we should 'anchor' some of our contemporary research in older moments of change in order to understand the present, just as it is important to undertake new research into audience histories to allow space for revisionism and to test our settled ideas of the past. It is important for us to do this in order to have any sense of the role of media in social and cultural change.

Chapter 3: 'Mean' asks the question, 'How should the researcher approach the overlapping processes of meaning-making?' This chapter opens with a scenario taken from the TV show Gogglebox (Channel 4) and revisits the key space generated by a sense of what audiences 'do' in inquiries into the 'active audience'. Whilst it understands meaning as operating through modes of interpretation, taken from earlier Cultural Studies, it also draws on useful insights from the 'uses and gratifications' tradition where they tell us something about the social order. It argues that we always need an expanded repertoire for understanding how audiences make meanings from media. Importantly, this chapter makes a case for the importance of questions of media 'form' which can help to open out analysis of our digital practices and experiences and becomes important to the model of 'the digital circuit' in Chapter 6.

Chapter 4: 'Feel' asks the question, 'What can feelings tell us about media audiences and changing social relations?' This chapter opens with a scenario about KPop fandom and argues that one important way into interrogating audiences has been to understand how media consumption is so tightly bound to the realm of emotions

INTRODUCTION 7

and feeling. This has a long tradition in Cultural Studies and moves through questions of audience' tastes and value, to the ways in which fan studies have explored the productive affective ties and bonds to media forms. It discusses the 'affective turn' in the social sciences and its usefulness to audience research in the current conjuncture. The chapter discusses 'contagious' feelings online in the analyses of 'affective publics' which can give us insights into contemporary citizenship and into the relationship between feelings and social change.

Chapter 5: 'Work' asks the question, 'Do audiences work?' This chapter opens with a scenario about the Creator Union in the UK and discusses the ways in which audience activity has been described as work beginning with early ideas from political economy about the audience as commodity. It then takes us into debates about audience labour and user-generated-content and considers some problematics for feminist research and its relationship to questions of social reproduction. In the digital landscape, now coupled with the acceleration of data extraction in order to 'know' audiences better, it considers the extent to which we should be considered 'workers' for platform capitalism. It describes the rise of ideas about 'work as life' and 'life as work' and how this is important to the rise of social media and 'influencing'.

Chapter 6: 'The Digital Circuit' asks the question, 'How should we adopt an "audience-sensitive" approach to digital culture for Cultural Studies?' The final chapter asks you to come up with your own scenario of a digital practice and works through these pathways in audience research to think about contemporary audience studies in an environment where audiencing is embedded across many digital cultural processes. It encourages the researcher to consider the 'warm bodies' that touch the screens and the keyboards in an attempt to hold onto lived experience. It takes Paul Du Gay (et al.'s) (1997/2013) 'the cultural circuit' and suggests that with the addition of 'form' into the circuit, we can operationalise a 'digital circuit' for use with a more complex set of techno-social relationships. All the time it is important to maintain the imperative of Cultural Studies' audience research to have some critical purchase on the current conjunctural moment and to ask the main question, 'what does this tell us about everything else?'.

A cursory study of the last ten years of some the main journals of Cultural Studies finds very little research that exactly uses the label audience studies. Yet a search for audience studies in undergraduate and postgraduate degree programs suggests that audience courses seem to be thriving, albeit with an important emphasis on participatory culture, or as closely allied to the key developments in fan studies. Much research, which might access what audiences feel or think is often derived from their enhanced visibility – the digital traces that they now leave online. But this textualisation of the audience often excludes the 'warm bodies' of lived experience. In the 1980s, Cultural Studies was critical of Film Studies' models of 'spectatorship' precisely because they could not evoke the real audience member sitting in front of the screen. There is a similar elision in some contemporary research that fills up a sense of audience or digital public with the marks they leave online sometimes without a sense of the body touching the keys or swiping the screen in the social and cultural conditions through which digital culture is lived. The main principle of this book therefore is to discourage research into digital practices from leap-frogging audience histories and their emphasis on culture as lived, and to approach a contemporary Cultural Studies of 'the digital circuit' in which lived experience is still central – because we are perceptive, sentient and toiling beings after all.

NOTE

1   https://www.ofcom.org.uk/news-centre/2022/living-our-lives-online (accessed April 6, 2023).

REFERENCES

Abercrombie, N. and Longhurst, B. (1998) *Audiences*. London: Sage.

Ang, I. (1991) *Desperately Seeking the Audience*. London and New York: Routledge.

Athique, A. (2016) *Transnational Audiences: Media Reception on a Global Scale*. London: Polity.

Du Gay, P., et al. (1997/2013) *Doing Cultural Studies: The Story of the Sony Walkman*. London: Sage.

Fiske, J. (1992) 'Audiencing: A cultural studies approach to watching television', *Poetics* 21: 345–359.

Gray, A. (2003) *Research Practice for Cultural Studies: Ethnographic Methods and Lived Cultures*. London: SAGE.

Williams, R. (2003) *Television Technology and Cultural Form* (3rd ed.). London and New York: Routledge Classics.

1

AUDIENCE

SCENARIO: THE CULT OF THE PELOTON FITNESS BIKE

During the Covid lockdown of 2020, the Peloton – basically a networked digitally enhanced exercise bike – took parts of the world by storm (Petter, 2020). Peloton's sales and profits during that period massively exploded, with a good deal of advertising, media attention and a celebrity-following which meant that it emerged as an iconic middle-class symbol of coping with crisis. So rapid and so intense was the take-up, of what is on the surface simply a fitness bike, it resulted in the phenomenon of 'Pelo' followers with their 'merch' and zealous commitment to the brand being described as a 'cult'. The word 'cult' follows around questions of media audiences since it conjures an over-intensive relationship with an object, a certain devotion and fandom that reaches levels of psychic obsession. I mention it here at the beginning of a book about audiences because of the way a number of relative, complex and overlapping issues coalesce around the Peloton fitness bike as a phenomenon.

There are many levels to the way in which the Peloton, as part of material-culture, is interesting for what it tells us about the

DOI: 10.4324/9781003414575-2

contemporary moment. Not least, the bike's position as a site of con-
spicuous consumption as users post images of the bike in their curated
personalised fitness rooms online as symbols of success. You can even
purchase a laptop tray for ultimate productivity so that working-
out can go hand-in-hand with paid work. The way in which the bike
operates with the accompanying platform allows the 'user' access to
an array of different fitness workouts from yoga and meditation to
power-zone workouts and core strength exercises. The fitness classes
themselves, viewed on the bike's screen, offer us a various array of
media texts, accompanied by carefully selected and themed music
sets, elevating the fitness instructors, their workout fashion and their
social media profiles to celebrity status.

There are a range of ways we can engage in relationships with the
instructors: there are 'shout-outs' to riders in live rides, as celebri-
ties we can follow their lives on Instagram, and send messages of
love and devotion, so much so that the word 'cult' does not seem too
far-fetched. The theming of rides and the motivational messages from
the instructors, all subscribe to a language of positivity and political
self-awareness. Rides for Black History Month, or Transawareness
day or 'body-positivity' also proffer a language of self-work and
empowerment.

The messages of individual self-love are registered with intense
feelings and commitment that also power the construction of its huge
and international digital community. As riders, you can see each
other on the leaderboard with your ride name; you can high-five each
other's performances which you can see and compete against, as you
hope to get a high-five from the instructor during the live-ride; and
most importantly you can join your favourite 'crew' and follow all
the socials. The Ladies Peloton Facebook group is a community of
women supporting each other through parenting difficulties, health
worries and errant partners all importantly with the right blouse and
wallpaper. Some groups even meet in-person, as riders claim that
they have found 'their' people and the group has 'changed lives'.
Of course, the cost of the bike and the monthly payments seem to
jar against the realities of the inequalities of the pandemic written
onto the bodies of working-class, black and ethnic minorities at the
front line and who are now facing another crisis in the rising costs
of living.

QUESTION: WHERE IS THE AUDIENCE HERE AND NOW?

Why have I started with this example of Peloton to begin a book about audiences? Are its members part of an 'audience' for Peloton, interpreting its messages of individual success? Or, are they simply 'users' making use of the bike simply to stay fit? Are they 'consumers', wanting to demonstrate conspicuous consumption, for their middle-class credentials and commitment to body-work? Or are they part of newly formed communities with associated interpersonal relationships through which they might move from a 'high-five' to a heart-felt friendship? Are they 'workers' for Peloton as they literally pedal traffic for the brand? The answer to *all* of these questions is yes because the bike positions the user/audience member/consumer/ friend, as all of these things all at once, and it is this hypercomplexity that characterises the contemporary media field for the study of audiences. In this chapter, I will set out for the emerging media audience researcher some of that complexity in order to shed light on the number of ways in which we might locate the lived bodies of audiences within our research.

Historically, as audience researchers interested in particular media or genre, we might simply have recruited the 'viewers', 'users', 'receivers', 'purchasers' and 'players' of those media forms as the objects of our analysis. The different ways audience engagements have been captured are also related to different media and academic histories, but for now let us assume a fairly straight-forward picture where potential audiences would have been approached as consumers of a relatively known set of outputs from a relatively limited number of media institutions. Those institutions were widely understood and relatively transparent in terms of their economic business models or public service affiliation and with that, their political leaning or sensibility. Those 'legacy' media institutions for all manner of reasons, related to the rise of the digital economy and the so-called democratisation of the media landscape, are under threat. Arguably so too is our ability to grasp a sense of 'the audience' as connected to a specified media output that will stand still long enough for us to study its formation and this has led to series of pleas to rejuvenate and regenerate audience research (Gray, 2017; Ytre-Arne and Das 2018;; Livingstone, 2019).

12 AUDIENCE

However, no one was ever only a member of one audience at any one time and this 'old' picture is still radically oversimplified. However, when we worked with discrete media or even discrete genre – at least, so we thought, we knew where to look for the media audiences of our media analysis. So where should we look for the audience now? How can we find audiences amongst the overlapping and ever complex explanations of the digital landscape? Fundamentally, in posing the question where is 'the audience', I am concerned with human social experience. Therefore, I will look through some of the more overarching accounts of techno-social change to see how the audience, that is characterised by warm bodies on the ground, is implied and figured, in order to give us some sensitising issues through which to feel our way through the field in later chapters. However, we must also be aware that this dominant narrative of techno-social change is most compatible with advanced capitalist societies – the Peloton bike is available in many but not all advanced capitalist nations. We must constantly check a media history that centres the West and be alive to the need for postcolonial 'interruptions' to challenge some of the normative temporalities which characterise technological developments from a particular vantage point (Shome, 2019).

AUDIENCES ARE MEDIATISED

To say that societies of advanced capitalism are increasingly 'media saturated' is of course a grave understatement; it simply does not capture the complexity of what that saturation means for society. John Thompson (1995) announced more than 25 years ago that the 'the media are like the air that we breathe' but we have since come even further whereby media forms now structure the fabric of our every existence in an 'always on' mentality of connection. We carry news, entertainment and social media around in our pockets such that media fill even the most-brief spaces of boredom. But the current relationship between media and society is more than a mode of continuous connection. What and whom are we connected to all this time? The ever-presence of media forms in most aspects of life mean that many of our other social processes – democracy, family, health, social care and education – are also transformed by the structured realities of their mediation. We can exist *within* media

AUDIENCE   13

and not always beyond their formation in what Mark Deuze (2012) has come to call 'media life'.

This point about the almost total absorption of social and cultural life into mediated processes has led to the characterisation, particularly in European theorising, of processes of 'mediation' or 'mediatisation'. This refers to the wider transformation of social and cultural life in a particular direction or what Altheide and Snow (1979) referred to, some time ago, as a 'media logic'. As Nick Couldry and Andrea Hepp (2017) argue, the very character of the social world is now constructed through mediated processes and infrastructures of communication. What we think of as 'the social', however problematic that term, is now already mediated.

Couldry and Hepp's take on this is less totalising than the idea of a complete 'media logic', because this depends on region, on specific historical developments of media governance, on the inequalities and politics of specific places and of course upon colonial histories. Therefore, mediatisation is not one smooth universal process or set of processes and it is not the outcome, solely, of digital infrastructures. Mediatisation is a dialectical process in any given society – not an entirely determining process than can be neatly predicted in any one site. It is rather, a terrain characterised by overlapping shifts as well as numerous technological developments, each of which have their own socio-political histories to tell.

Media studies, has however, often been concerned with producing macro accounts of media 'shifts' or what Couldry and Hepp (2017) characterise as waves: of mechanisation, electrification and digitalisation, pointing to a fourth wave: datafication. As Raka Shome argues (2019: 241) media studies tends towards a 'periodisation approach' but it is 'an approach which is situated in the temporal ordering orderings of North Atlantic modernity' (2019: 308). When we look for the audience in these waves, we are recounting a particular history. We might see our relationship to print and the early typewriter in the first phase, as readers; to later radio, telephony and television, as listeners and viewers, in the second wave of the broadcast era; as social media 'produsers' in the wave of digitalisation; and now as 'audience activity' which is recorded as aggregated algorithms in the landscape of datafication. These 'waves' are geographically dependent. For instance, Raka Shome (2019) tells of a different narrative related to the arrival of the press in India, as a disciplining rather than democratising technology under colonial rule, and challenges ideas of a linear narrative of progress.

From within such a dominant developmental narrative, it is tempting to think as though each new wave out-phases the last. But this is not so, media forms all still live on in mutated ways and our experiences as audiences co-exist, even if some are diminished and others are transformed, and are generationally and geographically dependant, in societies that are variously 'deeply' mediatised, dependent upon layers of media and mediated practice. The digital environment therefore relies on the intensified interrelatedness of many different media forms and contextual arrangements, enabled by the capacities of the internet in conditions that are now characterised by a kind of hypercomplexity. Such complexity has been more readily theorised in terms of overarching technological shifts and a narrative of change, but has been less easily documented 'on-the-ground' and in our lived experiences, which attends to questions of local and regional specificity.

AUDIENCES ARE PRODUSERS

A key aspect of digital complexity is that audiences are no longer entirely receivers of media, but also producers of media. Audiences can take part in some forms of media production, make and publish their own video material on sites like YouTube, generate forms of 'micro-celebrity' on Instagram and still perhaps interact with the directors of their favourite Bollywood film via X/Twitter, just as people might engage with their 'crew' on the Peloton. Boundaries that once kept producers and audiences apart are eroded (Lind, 2015) – although it is also fair to say that new boundaries are emerging, and we should be cautious of any over-easy celebration of democratisation. These conditions are enabled by the convergence of what were once separate media forms and new platforms for interactivity, moving away from what were once one-way modes of communication.

These conditions of 'convergence culture' (Jenkins, 2008) position audiences in myriad ways. Similar forms or texts – print, TV, film and so on – still exist in recognisable forms, but their systems of delivery via online digital platforms mean we can stream, download and engage with media in numerous, and also continually evolving, platform architectures. The *forms* of delivery and the new interfaces and audience engagements that they generate are important. In some ways, newer media forms have so much potential for more democratic and participatory models of media engagement, now that mass communication has merged with peer-to-peer communication – mass media and social media co-exist and interact just as they do on the Peloton fitness bike. Here the once stable categories of 'producer' and 'user' have been completely undermined, producing new categories like 'produser' (Bruns, 2009) which captures the now conflated categories whereby one can consume a media text, alter it, remake it and share it via alternative platforms. Although it is also important to note that examples of 'produsage' existed before the advent of the internet. For instance, see discussions of the activities of radio enthusiasts building their own hobby sets, or diaspora communities' innovative approaches to video-production and distribution (Moores, 1988; Naficy, 1993) of which we must continually remind ourselves as we circle-back to learn from alternative histories in our attempts to understand technological transformation. (see Chapter 2).

Older traditional media institutions, like the BBC or CNN have their own YouTube channels in order to reach larger audiences which captures a very important character of digital culture: its propensity towards 'context collapse'. Audiences are navigating a multi-layered set of experiences at any one time. Now *trans*mediality characterises the media landscape and transforms older media forms. For instance, Elisabeth Evans (2013) discusses the ways in which new multiplatform strategies generate multi-screen experiences for television audiences. What were once distinct media forms (TV, film) sit side-by-side just one click away from each other. What were once distant actors in older media worlds – stars, directors – sit side-by-side with 'ordinary' audience members commentating on the latest release. This collapse represents the ability to move away from medium-specific content towards multiple ways of accessing and distributing media content 'and toward ever more complex relations between top-down corporate media and bottom-up participatory culture' (Jenkins, 2008: 243).

For some these old hierarchies generated via the concentration of media ownership are crumbling in a potential flattening of the

16 AUDIENCE

apparatus of delivery away from linear modes of transmission into this more diffuse set of networked media. This context has generated a feeling that the mainstream media have lost control of 'the audience' and refers to 'the people formally known as the audience' (Rosen, 2008: 163) in this shift from 'one-to-many' (mass) to 'many-to-many' (peer) – enabling their activities whilst simultaneously making them less identifiable. When audiences can create their own media (videos, gifs, images, manga) and distribute it with relative ease there has been an assumption that 'user-generated content' is the panacea for a more egalitarian model of media access and distribution, jettisoning from the 'old' debates the traditional dichotomies of 'active-passive' and 'macro and micro' audience models. Whilst the meaning of this term (UGC) might seem clear – content produced by users – as a category even this is an umbrella term for lots of different types of activity, from blogs to wikis, podcasting, video-sharing, file-sharing and so on. Audience activity is thus now a multitude of different practices but they are not necessarily entirely detached from the precedents in legacy media. As Nico Carpentier reminds us, the key distinction lies in the range of *modality* rather than their actual novelty in 'an intensification and massafication of already existing participatory practices' (Carpentier, 2014: 206). By 'modality' he is referring to the particular form or means that media take in their address to, or relationship with, audiences, which will become an important concern for this book.

Some of the more optimistic rendering of these debates about participatory culture are located in the promise of participation itself. But is this necessarily participation that makes any difference at all to the maintenance of a better-informed democracy? There has been a hopefulness embedded in early thinking about the disruptive potential of the internet, because of the very agentive nature of the network itself (Castells, 2009) in what Curran, Fenton and Freedman (2012) refer to the as the 'internet of dreams' (2012: 1). And indeed this seemed to be borne out by the Arab Spring uprisings of 2011 in Egypt – the so-called 'Twitter Revolutions' whereby Castells (2012: 1 cited in Curran) proclaimed 'dictatorships could be overthrown with the bare hands of the people'. Similarly, we might want to think of the #MeToo moment when the groundswell of women's feeling about sexual violence generated a platform for change particularly in Hollywood (Boyle, 2019). Anti-racist diasporic groups have used 'digitised tactics' to raise awareness in order to fight oppression across the globe (Kumar, 2018). In these contexts, digital media audiences can also occupy another role as 'activists' using media technologies as the instruments for social justice and change. Connectivity can therefore offer huge benefits generating a 'digital diaspora' of dispersed populations, where digital connectivity has transformed the terms of spaciality and belonging (Ponzanesi, 2020). Other work on connectivity and migration shows how digital spaces offer generative spaces for the performance of identity and belonging (Leurs, 2012) all of which suggests the potential gains made through the tools of 'produsage'.

There have also been more sober evaluations of the role of social media in the functioning of democracies. Zizi Papacharissi (2010: 131) outlines how 'Contemporary civic actions are characterised by a variety of atomised action, taking place in a plurality of spaces that are both private and public.' This kind of work cautions us against a techno-determinist approach to media – and by extension audiences – through which we read what is happening through the potential of the technology. We should remember media are imbued with the uneven socio-political and cultural contexts in which they emerge that are not necessarily pre-determined by the inherent nature of the technology itself. It seems that as audiences, we have latent potential, with some of the instruments in our hands for potential change. But the contexts which take into account the histories and geographies in which change might occur are all important and we must insist on interrogating them too if we are interested in the social life of audiences.

AUDIENCES ARE WORKERS

There is no doubt that access to multiple forms of media has greatly opened up during these more recent technological waves of digitalisation in a vastly proliferated and abundant immersive media environment. If we already had more than enough – then potentially now – is it all too much? It is interesting to note now that many people are permanently connected through personalised mobile media that we speak of the need to 'unplug' or even 'detox' especially from social media's constancy in our everyday lives as a mode of resistance (Syvertsen,

2020). Although this must still be tempered by the acknowledgement that in some parts of the world the irregularity of the electricity supply directly interrupts any universal sense of 'always on' (Shome, 2019). Sherry Turkle (2012) became so cautious of this environment where social relations had moved online that she fears that we come to expect more of technology and less of each other, jeopardising interpersonal face-to-face conversation and more 'authentic' human-social relations. I have discussed elsewhere how there are problems in seeing this as an entirely zero-sum game without accounting for the depth and range of mediated and social experiences and of course of their highly contextualised and contingent nature (Wood, 2010).

Arguably we need to understand this media complexity as it is tied to the changing nature of work in advanced capitalist societies and these changing conditions have seen a return to media and audience studies of the Marxist theorising of the Frankfurt school, whereby entertainment was seen the prolongation of work under late capitalism (Adorno and Horkheimer, 1944). These claims seem more pressing now than ever with the increased precarity of working lives and the encroachment of working practices into our leisure time. Online forms of work (emails, zoom meetings, google calendar scheduling) or the affective work of maintaining your social media presence (for growing your 'reputation' for your business, service or just lifestyle) have collapsed a series of boundaries – just like working-at-home during your workout in the example of the Peloton above. This challenges boundaries not only between the private and the public (a process of course which began with much earlier legacy media forms), but also between work and home and work and leisure. This applies even if we are not 'social media influencers' where personal lifestyling through media *is* work (see Chapter 5). The 'gig economy' that the so-called generation of 'digital natives' inhabit is enabled by the platforms which gamify the nature of much work, from taxi-driving to pizza delivery and even to GP services (see Jarrett, 2022). The fuel to succeed in such a dizzying environment is generated by an ideological call to 'do what you love' as part of the creation of an ideal neoliberal subject (who in all likelihood works-out whilst they answer their emails). This ultimately has an effect upon our sense of time as the register of work's new intimacy exploits the pact between emotional and temporal investments (Greig, 2012) and we are fundamentally implored to 'do more' for success.

In this re-ordering of space and time, where the apparent freedoms and pleasures offered by entertainment media come to us via the same devices as our work emails, 'time' itself becomes the greatest commodity. We experience this time pressure not only in relation to the abundant calls on our attention, but as what Harmut Rosa (2015) identifies more broadly as social acceleration: the quickening tempo of modern social life in part brought about by technological change. As Sarah Sharma has argued, there exists large differences in our relationships with time that 'organise and perpetuate inequalities' (2015: 137) and by extension influence any experience of being part of an 'audience'. Newer working practices in some of the so-called advanced economies rely on intensive, heavily monitored and self-actualised time-management systems which are punitive at the same time as they absolve employers from any form of responsibility – for instance in the case of carers and delivery drivers. Whilst platforms themselves gesture towards openness and accessibility, these forms of labour are gendered, raced and classed and ensconced in colonial histories and are fundamental to the ways in which mediatised societies are also deeply unequal. Therefore, we must pay attention to the way 'audiences' exist at the boundaries of our working lives that are baked into uneven social structures, whether or not we characterise audience behaviour precisely as 'work' (see Chapter 5).

AUDIENCES ARE NEOLIBERAL

The constant pulls upon our time and energy for consumption, entertainment and work (areas that now bleed into one another) are compounded by the added pressures to practice greater introspection and self-evaluation in advanced capitalist economies which espouse neoliberal ideologies of competition, enterprise and meritocracy (Littler, 2018). This kind of 'entrepreneurialism' of the self is intensified by the 24×7 media culture of constant and instant connection. This experience is also highly gendered, as Ros Gill (2017) has detailed extensively in terms of the advances of a postfeminist call to self-improvement that dovetails with the neoliberal imperative to constantly improve. For instance, consider the amount of mediated calls to beauty-work and self-work appear in the name of 'confidence' across lifestyle media.

As Gill and Orgad (2020) point out 'confidence culture' presses on women at the same time that their rising numbers in the workplace and the boardroom are not met by the necessary provision of child-care resources. These imperatives also divide women in terms of class and race because of distinctions between those that have the resources to take part and those that do not. These are distinctions that have been exacerbated by austerity culture and an 'anti-welfareism' particularly in the UK (McRobbie, 2020). Even more damagingly, the constant mantra of the neoliberal ideologies of self-work, resilience and self-reliance have potentially secured consent for the withdrawal of the welfare contract, thereby framing those most in need in our society as failures and even fraudsters.

The media's intensified role in our narratives of self-work are often teased out in media analyses of texts and forms, but we also need to understand the ways in which they reach audiences. For instance, postfeminism has often been discussed as though it assumes a white middle-class subject, but Simidele Dosekun's (2020) work that draws on interviews with wealthy Nigerian women in Lagos discusses how their spectacular femininity also orients them towards similar individualised empowerment narratives in a more transnational account of postfeminism. In fact, Wendy Willems (2014) argues that an entry point such as processes like neoliberalism might be a better way through which to de-centre dominant Western narratives than to focus on media systems. We therefore need to think more about how audiences are experiencing the intensities of these mediated and cultural processes on the ground. How do audiences make and interpret meaning in a range of contexts? How does neoliberalism generate 'structures of feeling' in audiences, as we will discuss in Chapter 4. Importantly, how are different groups positioned in relation to these intensities and what impact does this have on questions of identity? All questions that are vital to audience research precisely because of what is politically at stake in our analysis.

AUDIENCES ARE DATA

Connected audiences are immersed in an 'attention economy' that gets us to stay, read, click, post and (hopefully) buy – just as in the all-absorbing landscape of the cult of the Peloton fitness bike. This involves a targeted and lucrative science gathering the neuroscientists to better monitor and even shepherd the online audience in consumer aggregating, tracking and quantification. How to deal with this from the point of the view of 'the audience'? Traditionally Cultural Studies research into the relationship between audience activity and capitalism would have been focussed on the level of ideology; the ways in which media messages tend to reinforce ideas about the status quo as outlined above (see Chapter 3). The audience figured most prominently in terms of understanding how messages were interpreted, generating consent for the ways in which society is unevenly structured through the means of capital. But audiences themselves have a longer history of also being important commodities in commercial exchange. I discuss in Chapter 5 the ways in which audiences are useful as metrics in delivering numbers to advertisers in the interests of capital. In this current more 'immersive' picture outlined above, audience activity and behaviour has become the raw data of capital accumulation. According to Nick Srnicke (2017: 40) 'Simply put we should consider data to be the raw material that must be extracted and the activities of users to be the natural source of this raw material'. In this game, the owners of this new source of revenue are the owners of the platforms that provide the overarching digital infrastructures which generate and foster interaction. For Melissa Gregg and Dawn Nafus (2017) the obsession with data analytics represents, 'the last gasp of participatory media' as we have less and less control over our relationships to data (cited in Andrejevic, 2014).

Platforms therefore position themselves between 'users' as the very ground upon which interactions occur. They are subject to what are called 'network effects' in that they become more effective the more users they have which has seen the dominance of Facebook and Instragram (and now TikTok) as preeminent social media sites and Google as the preeminent search engine tending towards monopolisation (Srnicke, 2017). As platforms can accrue many activities and many users to their sites this means they seem to have few limits to their expansion. Any sense of 'audiences' are therefore mostly useful to capital in their numbers. Information as data about audience/user activities across these platforms can be mined and sold to other parties in order to better target more selling and more content, which means that the major profits of key platforms come from advertising revenue.

This has led to critical theorists concerned about the exploitation of the 'free labour' of audiences, where 'users are unwaged labourers who produce goods (data and content) that are taken and sold by the companies to advertisers and other interested parties' (Srnicke, 2017: 53, for a lengthier discussion see Chapter 5).

This situation has been called 'surveillance capitalism' (Zuboff, 2019) with associated concerns for transgressions in our privacy and human rights. Or a situation of 'data colonialism' which 'makes the entirety of our existence available to capitalism' (Couldry and Mejias, 2019: 86/87).

AUDIENCES ARE THE WARM BODIES

My training in Cultural Studies has meant that I have often asked the question 'where are the warm bodies?' when faced with this picture of transformation and change in media studies, that has tended to talk of 'users' instead of 'audiences', and of seismic shifts driven from readings of technology rather than what is happening 'on-the-ground'. Where are real people in this picture? Have we simply disappeared into our ability to be aggregated into a number of clicks? As Adrian Athique (2018) reminds us, audiences are NOT data. To counter some of the technological and economically-determinist impulses in the theorising of the subsumption of social and human relations to data – we surely need to grasp the complexity and diversity of human experience, especially if we want to martial any resistive potential, as Cultural Studies would want to do.

As Paul Dourish (2016) has argued algorithms are not static, they are always situated, and there are some similarities here with the shift that established the 'active audience' tradition in media audience research. The 'active audience' tradition was in a large part driven by Cultural Studies as a response to the more administrative, governmental and commercial imperative of direct 'effects' research (see Chapter 2). Early encounters with 'real' audiences tended to challenge the assumptions of effects research in messy and conflicting ways. But there has not yet been a concerted enough response from qualitative social scientists and humanities-based research to the question of big data as a social process, a fact which is 'hardly helpful to those who want to defend the role of human agency in the world' (Couldry and Mejias, 2019: 142).

We must therefore understand the ways in which audiences are 'tethered' to the data world through their lived experiences. Helen Kennedy (2018) has argued that we must always speak to people in order to think through the ways in which living with data has become 'ordinary', drawing from Cultural Studies' accounts of that term to argue for a greater focus on living with data. She suggests that this is doubly important if we want to explore the possibilities of data activism and data justice – understanding people's emotional engagements with data to identify their nascent resistive potential. Examples of work with communities and groups to better understand their relationship to data include Couldry, Fotopoulou, and Dickens's (2016) Storycircle project examining the use of data analytics with community groups, and Taina Bucher's (2017) work on what social media users feel about the use of platforms and their algorithms. Couldry and Mejias (2019) at the end of their book point us to their algorithm observatory (https://ulisesmejias.com/algorithm-observatory/) – the goal of which is: 'to give the general public simple and accessible resources to understand how social-computing algorithms categorize us' (p. 210) and recent work in Pink et al.'s (eds) (2022) *Everyday Automation* offers a 'people-focussed' approach to algorithms and automation.

However, these studies are not often thought about as having a relationship with previous audience research and yet as Sonia Livingstone (2019), in her analysis of audience studies in an age of datafication has pointed out, there are important lessons to be learned from its histories. First, what is said about audiences is always open to question. Second, audiences are never as gullible as they are presented, largely because they are not homogenous or uncritical, and finally that we need to reassert that there is no simple binary between media power and audience power. Livingstone (2019) comes back to the Cultural Studies model of the 'circuit of culture' (Du Gay et al., 1997) which is an important move, and one which I will return to in Chapter 6 of this book. This is important because in the now many macro accounts of data societies they can be read as though we live without culture, contexts and identities at all. For instance, Livingstone (2019) critiques the way theorisations of 'mediatisation' and 'datafication' obscure the documentation of the 'lifeworld'. In macro accounts of grander social paradigm shifts, technological and economic models drive the theory, whilst the details of what people actually do from

24 AUDIENCE

their multifarious range of social and cultural locations is key to any fundamental understanding of audience activity.

The 'circuit of culture' (Du Gay et al., 1997) is important for considering the interrelationships between five key processes in the formation of culture: consumption, production, representation, regulation and identity. In Chapter 6, I suggest that we can come back to that model for digital culture, but with the addition of another cultural process 'form'. This is to consider the importance of modalities to the questions of the circulation of meaning which can also cope with the plethora of new user interfaces, platforms and digital engagements that are on offer in digital culture. This is in order to better grasp the workings of power and inequality and not as a functional systems approach to the circulation of meaning.

Whilst it might seem like data algorithms operate without an ideology, 'networks without a cause' (Lovink, 2012), it has become clear that they operate with social and historically-primed injustices embedded in their architectures. For instance, as in Safiya Noble's account of the racist 'algorithms of oppression', or Virginia Eubanks (2017) analysis of the way internet architectures structure a 'digital poorhouse' or my analysis of the transference of classed disgust via clickbait (Wood, 2018). Their impact upon social life is meaning-*full*. The role of social contexts in the digital circulation of meaning and how 'warm bodies' are encouraged to enact, manage, negotiate and possibly even resist power and injustice are of course the concerns that have always been at the heart of Cultural Studies approaches to audiences.

AUDIENCING: A CONJUNCTURAL ANALYSIS

Media and cultural studies can easily cope with these shifts if we circle-back and use John Fiske's (1992) suggestion that instead of looking for 'the audience' we might turn our attention towards audience as a verb: 'to audience'. Fiske drew this term from his analyses of television viewing in the nineties when television audience research was at the centre of mainstream of media studies and in dialogue with more positivistic approaches to measuring audiences. He makes an argument for the social formation of audiences that can cope with a set of complex and overlapping social and cultural contexts through which formations coalesce around media *forms* and texts, 'a social formation is formed and dissolved more fluidly around its contextual conditions. It is identified by what its members do rather than by what they are, and as such it is better able to account non-reductively for the complexities and contradictions in everyday life in a highly elaborated society' (1992: 350/1).

Here I want to expand on Fiske's proposition of 'audiencing' as it helps us to think of social practices; offering us ways to draw out the systemic relationships of our media engagements with wider social contexts. The key challenge that I outlined above around the Peloton is the multiplicity of ways in which we engage across media in a highly complex digital environment. This is a 'composite' environment, which means that audiences are navigating a densely populated 'polymedia' landscape (Madianou, 2014). Fiske's 1992 study of students watching television in a room as social glue might now be a more physically dispersed experience accompanied by social media connections, posting and debating the programme with a much wider audience. Then as now: 'The system by which meanings are circulated in a society resembles a maelstrom rather than an engineering diagram' (1992: 359).

The central proposition for Cultural Studies has *always* been to work through the complexities of a cultural world in which we must pay attention to the overlapping formations of the textual, technological, social, economic and political. Lawrence Grossberg refers to such an approach as 'radical contextualisation' (2010) – a particular effort to understand the complexity of 'what's going on' through a sustained commitment to the particular moment in which it occurs. This is what is termed a 'conjunctural analysis'. As Jeremy Gilbert (2019: 6) outlines, a conjunctural analysis, 'can be broadly defined as the analysis of convergent and divergent tendencies shaping the totality of power relations within a given social field during a particular period of time'.

Audience analysis of course has to evolve to explore the complexity of the conjunctural moment, which is not always set by the pace of technological advancement, but also by the entwined forces of social, political and cultural change. Therefore, when we study the audience from a Cultural Studies perspective, we MUST ask questions about 'what does this tell us about everything else?' When I think about the

26 AUDIENCE

Peloton audience, I have to ask a number of questions about what it tells me: How do we need to connect and find community in a context of isolation and individualism? How are we understanding these messages and ideologies of self-work in a neoliberal landscape? How do these para-social relationships with celebrity fitness instructors work? Who is included and excluded in this privileged community? These would be the questions that would inform an audience research project with the Peloton 'users' and then I could test out my suspicions around an overall digital circuit which I will come back to in Chapter 6. I cannot know this without coming into contact with the 'warm – now also hot and sweaty – bodies' and without understanding their social and cultural contexts, or without some kind of empirical understanding of the ways in which their lived realities are tethered to the physical/digital relationships and social formations that are activated by the multimedia bike. Bring forth the maelstrom.

CONCLUSION

I started this chapter by asking, *Where is the audience here and now?* Which has not resulted in a coherent set of answers, but rather a set of overarching frameworks that need testing on the ground. This chapter has mapped the relatively recent and accelerated changed sets of circumstances that the audience researcher now must take into account. By opening with the Peloton fitness bike it presented something of the complexity that media and cultural forms now involve in their articulations with audiences in the digital circuit. It has therefore taken on board the current conjuncture that is characterised by a hypercomplex digital environment. It has teased out where the audience *is* in the more abstract theoretical descriptions of change from mass media to participatory media and to datafied societies, pointing out that audiences are often barely implicitly drawn within some of these grand narratives of rapid technological change. Informed by others such as Sonia Livingstone (2019) and Ytre-Arne and Ranjana Das (2018), I join Jonathan Gray's (2017: 83) call 'to repopulate media studies scholarship more fully with humanity, people and culture' through contemporary audiences studies.

We can stay with the concept 'audiencing' as a way to theorise and make sense of the radically contextual conditions of contemporary societies that can account for the rapid and intensified changes of the kind outlined above. Such a contextual account can cope with the hypercomplexity of the current conjuncture – that is how an approach to 'audiencing', which can draw the lines between (macro) social and technical structures and (micro) local conditions and experiences, has always worked. In the next chapter, I suggest that one of the ways to do that well is by holding on to some of the lessons of audience research (Livingstone, 2019) and to point to places where the contemporary conjuncture might invite us to 'circle-back' and learn from the histories of the field (Chapter 2).

REFERENCES

Adorno, T. and Horkeimer, A. (1944/2012) 'The culture industry: Enlightenment as mass deception', reprinted in Durham, M. and Kellner, D.M. (eds.) *Media and Cultural Studies: Keyworks* (2nd ed., KeyWorks in Cultural Studies). Hoboken, NJ: John Wiley & Sons, Incorporated 94–136.

Altheide, D.L. and Snow, R.P. (1979) *Media Logic*. London and New York: Sage.

Andrejevic, M. (2014) 'The big data divide', *International Journal of Communication* 8 (17): 1673–1689.

Athique, A. (2018) 'The dynamics and potentials of big data for audience research', *Media, Culture & Society* 40 (1): 59–74. https://doi-org.ezproxy.lancs. ac.uk/10.1177/0163443717693681

Boyle, K. (2019) *MeToo, Weinstein and Feminism*. Cham: Springer International Publishing.

Bruns, A. (2009) 'From Prosumer to Produser: Understanding User-Led Content Creation'. Paper presented at Transforming Audiences Conference London September 2009. https://eprints.qut.edu.au/27370/

Bucher, T. (2017) 'The algorithmic imaginary: exploring the ordinary affects of Facebook algorithms', *Information, Communication & Society* 20 (1): 30–44, https://doi.org/10.1080/1369118X.2016.1154086

Carpentier, N. (2014) 'New configurations of the audience? The challenges of user generated content for audience theory and media participation', in Nightingale, V. (ed.) *The Handbook of Media Audiences*. Chichester: Wiley Blackman, pp. 190–212.

Castells, M. (2009) *The Rise of the Network Society*. London: Wiley.

Couldry, N., Fotopoulou, A., and Dickens, L. (2016) 'Real social analytics: A contribution towards a phenomenology of a digital world', *The British Journal of Sociology* 67 (1): 118–137.

Couldry, N. and Hepp, A. (2017) *The Mediated Construction of Reality*. London: Polity Press.

Couldry, N. and Mejias, U. (2019) *The Costs of Connection: How data is colonising human life and Appropriating it for Capitalism*. Stanford, CA: Stanford University Press.

28 AUDIENCE

Curran, J., Fenton, N., and Freeman, D. (2012) *Misunderstanding the Internet*. London: Routledge.

Deuze, M. (2012) *Media Life*. London: Polity.

Dosekun, S. (2020) *Fashioning postfeminism: Spectacular femininity and transnational culture*. Dissident Feminisms Ser. Champaign: University of Illinois Press.

Dourish, P. (2016) 'Algorithms and their others: Algorithmic culture in context', *Big Data & Society*. https://doi.org/10.1177/2053951716665128

Du Gay, P., et al. (1997) *Doing Cultural Studies: The Story of the Sony Walkman*. London: Sage.

Eubanks, V. (2017) *Automating Inequality: How High Tech Tools, Profile, Police and Punish the Poor*. New York: St Martin's Press.

Evans, E. (2013) *Transmedia Television Audiences, New Media, and Daily Life*. London and New York: Routledge.

Fiske, J. (1992) 'Audiencing: A cultural studies approach to watching television', *Poetics* 21: 345–359.

Gill, R. (2017) 'The affective, cultural and psychic life of postfeminism: A postfeminist sensibility 10 years on', *European Journal of Cultural Studies* 20 (6): 606–626. https://doi.org/10.1177/1367549417733003

Gill, R. and Orgad, S. (2022) *Confidence Culture* Chapel Hill, Duke University Press.

Gilbert, J. (2019) 'This conjuncture: For Stuart Hall', *New Formations: A Journal of Culture/Theory/Politics* 96–97: 5–37.

Gray, J. (2017) 'Reviving audience studies', *Critical Studies in Media Communication* 34 (1): 79–83.

Greig, M. (2012) *Work's Intimacy*. Cambridge: Polity Press.

Gregg, M. and Nafus, D. (2017) 'Data', in Ouellette, L. and Gray, J. (eds.) *Keywords for Media Studies*. New York: New York University Press, pp. 55–70.

Grossberg, L. (2010) *Cultural Studies in the Future Tense*. Durham: Duke University Press.

Jarrett, K. (2022) *Digital Labour*. Cambridge: Polity.

Jenkins, H. (2008) *Convergence Culture: Where Old and New Media Collide*. New York: New York University Press.

Kennedy, H. (2018) 'Living with data: Aligning data studies and data activism through a focus on everyday experiences of datafication', *Krisis: Journal for Contemporary Philosophy* 1: 18–30.

Kumar, P. (2018) 'Re-routing the narrative: Mapping the online identity politics of the Tamil and Palestinian diaspora', *Social Media+Society* 4 (1): 205630511876442.

Leurs, K. (2012) *Digital Passages: Morrocan-Dutch Youths Performing Diapora, Gender and Youth Cultural Identities across Digital Space*. Amsterdam: Amsterdam University Press.

Lind, R.A. (ed.). (2015) *Produsing Theory in a Digital World 2.0: The Intersection of Audiences and Production in Contemporary Theory*, Vol. 2. New York: Peter Lang.

Littler, J. (2018) *Against Meritocracy: Culture, Power and Myths of Mobility*. Abingdon, Oxon; NewYork: Routledge.

Livingstone, S. (2019) 'Audiences in an age of datafication: Critical questions of media research', *Television and New Media* 20 (2): 170–183.

AUDIENCE **29**

Lovink, G. (2012) *Networks without a Cause*. Cambridge: Polity.

Madianou, M. (2014) 'Polymedia communication and mediatized migration: an ethnographic approach', in Knut Lundby (ed.) *Mediatization of Communication*. Berlin: DE GRUYTER, pp. 323–348.

McRobbie, A. (2020) *Feminism and the Politics of Resilience: Essays on Gender, Media and the End of Welfare*. Cambridge: Polity Press.

Moores, S. (1988). 'The box on the dresser': Memories of early radio and everyday life. *Media, Culture & Society* 10 (1), 23–40. https://doi.org/10.1177/016344388010001003

Naficy, H. (1993) *The Making of Exile Cultures: Iranian Television in Los Angeles*. Minnesota, University of Minnesota Press.

Papacharissi, Z. (2010) *A Private Sphere: Democracy in a Digital Age* (1st ed.). Digital Media and Society Ser. Oxford: Polity Press.

Petter, O. (2020) 'The cult of Peloton: How an at-home spinning community became a pandemic obsession'. Available at: https://www.independent.co.uk/life-style/peloton-lockdown-instructors-change-lives-b1759232.html (accessed June 16, 2023).

Ponzanesi, S. (2020) 'Digital diasporas: Postcoloniality, media and affect', *Interventions* 22 (8): 977–993. https://doi.org/10.1080/1369801X.2020.1718537

Rosa, H. (2015) *Social Acceleration: A New Theory of Modernity*. New York: Columbia University Press.

Rosen, J. (2008) 'The people formally known as the audience', in Carpentier, N. and De Cleen, B. (eds.) *Participation and Media Production: Critical Reflections on Content Creation*. Newcastle: Cambridge Scholars, pp. 163–165.

Sharma, S. (2015) *In the Meantime: Temporality and Cultural Politics*. Durham, NC: Duke University Press.

Shome, R. (2019) 'When postcolonial studies interrupts media studies', *Communication, Culture and Critique* 12: 305–322.

Srnicke, N. (2017) *Platform Capitalism*. London: Polity.

Syvertsen, T. (2020) *Digital Detox: The Politics of Disconnecting*. First ed. Bingley: Emerald Publishing (SocietyNow).

Thompson, J. (1995) *The Media and Modernity: A Social Theory of the Media*. Cambridge: Polity Press.

Turkle, S. (2012) *Alone Together: Why We Expect More from Technology and Less from Each Other*. New York: Basic Books.

Willems, W. (2014) 'Beyond normative dewesternization: Examining media culture from the vantage point of the global south', *The Global South* 8 (1): 7–23.

Wood, H. (2010) 'From Media and Identity to Mediated Identity', in Wetherell, M. and Mohanty, C.T. (eds.) *The Sage Handbook of Identities*. Sage: London and New York, pp. 258–276.

Wood, H. (2018) 'The Magaluf Girl: A public sex scandal and the digital class relations of social contagion', *Feminist Media Studies* [Special issue on 'Online Misogyny', Ging, D. and Siapera, E. (eds.)] 8 (4): 626–642.

Ytre-Arne, B. and Das, R. (2018) 'An agenda in the interest of audiences: Facing the challenges of intrusive media technologies', *Television and New Media* 20 (2): 184–198.

Zuboff, S. (2019) *The Age of Surveillance Capitalism: The Fight for a Human Future at the New Frontier of Power*. London: Profile Books.

2

ANCHOR

SCENARIO: 'HOUSEWIFE AGED 18'

In my archival research into historical media audiences, I visited the Mass Observation Archives[1] at The Keep in Sussex UK. One of the things that I found most powerful about having conducted archival research into women's reception of early television is the proximity it gave me to young women living in the post-war era in Britain. In my first visit to the Mass Observation archives, I vividly remember the range of emotions that were conjured up as I held hand-written accounts of women in the 1940s who were thinking about the prospect of acquiring a television set (see Wood, 2015). I really felt the distinction between my life and theirs as I lifted out their beautifully written accounts of the fears, as well as the occasional excitement, at the prospect of a television set.[2] Many of them were concerned about the distraction that television might pose to their daily domestic working lives of needlework, cooking, cleaning, against their description of themselves as (for example) 'housewife aged 18'.

As a feminist television studies scholar, at the archive, it felt important to lift out those voices from the 1940s and to register their

DOI: 10.4324/9781003414575-3

ANCHOR   31

vibrant, and often politicised views, then and a little later when they considered commercial television (see Wood and Kay, 2021). It makes me certain of the value of drawing out the lineages of the political, social and cultural distinctions between then and now and the place that media has taken up in its relationship with social change.

Thinking about 'Housewife age 18' worried about a TV set compared to the accounts of (some – privileged and often white) girls performing themselves with such apparent confidence on Tik-Tok (Kennedy, 2020) tells us something of the distance travelled in between early television of the 1940s and Tik-Tok of the 2020s. The young girl in the 1940s resisted television because it did not give her enough time to take pride in her newly achieved home – this was important as social housing and changes from roles of service meant that increasingly more 'ordinary' women could take pride in household management. Zoom forward today, to the young girl goofing around in her bedroom at her parent's house in front of her phone filming her hundredth video of the day, carefully curating an image of a lifestyle often based around consumption, and not working on the chores of domesticity. Of course, these girls do not stand in for all girls and their contextually-dependant relationships with media – which is important for us to register. For me, though, the figures of these two girls are important because of what they tell us, in the spirit of Cultural Studies, about everything else. They both centre the grand narratives that were mentioned in the last chapter, but also fill them up with the importance of context and of warm bodies, and gives us some insights with which to trouble some of our dominant narratives in the field, as I will come back to later in this chapter.

QUESTION: HOW CAN AUDIENCE HISTORIES HELP US TO UNDERSTAND SOCIAL CHANGE?

After the last chapter's discussion of the audience in the development of the digital age, I use the example above to remind us of the importance of historicising the audience, keeping the past always in tension with our present theorising. Of course, we do not have a complete understanding the media's relationship with social change since it

32 ANCHOR

involves such a complex set of relations. What we have at our disposal is a set of histories of the way we have been able to 'see' and to 'know' audiences in particular ways. Audiences have been brought into view for political reasons at particular socio-historical junctures and these developments are influenced by the changing landscape of academic (and a dominance of Anglo-American) ways of thinking. Richard Butsche and Sonia Livingstone (2015) have encouraged us to produce more transnational and comparative accounts of the ways audiences are 'known' through discourse, not only in the ongoing project to 'de-westernise' media studies, but also to do the work of translation, 'to communicate the nuance of context, and holistic experiences of one culture to those from another culture' (2015: 2). There is not space here to do full justice to the breadth of audience analysis from a range of disciplinary spaces and locations, but it is still important for the audience researcher to understand when and how different audience analyses have emerged in order to fully 'anchor' our contemporary research.

One of the imperatives of this book is that there is a continuous need to do some 'circling back', in order to move forward, with a caution not to be driven *only* by technological change. We should be reminded of the need technological determinism in which: '[n]ew technologies are discovered by an essentially internal process of research and development, which then sets the conditions for social change and progress' (Williams, 1974: 13). It is a common tendency to see media technologies as the driving forces of change, rather than as subject to the complex arrangements of social, cultural and economic formations. Technological developments do, of course to some extent, set and create new conditions for audiences as we have seen in the last chapter, but by always attending to *audience*, as well as the technology, we can privilege the contextual and the social in order to avoid such a determinist position. An understanding of the past, and past audiences, will also to help us to make sense of the present and future media landscape because there are traces and lineages to be borne in mind whenever we attend to any new phenomena.

'Audiencing' retains some consistency over time since being part of an audience predates what we might think of as the 'mass media', 'networked media' or 'platform media' and is an inherently *social* phenomenon. Just as we must use learning from the past to help make

ANCHOR 33

sense of the present, so too must we look in the other direction and use the developments of the field to look back at settled accounts and generate space for revisionism, which must also be part of any decolonising project. The final section, therefore, will show the value of contemporary historical audience research, of continuing to flesh out accounts of historical transition, and of always assuming that our work on a phenomenon or medium is not done, just because the technology has moved on.

WAYS OF SEEING AUDIENCES

Perspectives on audiences have often stemmed from social concerns over their very presence: bringing audiences into existence by the very the act of describing fears for 'other' people. It has often been repeated that audiences are not 'real'; they are 'invisible fictions' (Hartley, 1992) generated by those seeking knowledge about them. The history of the audience is to some extent the history of 'the people': of their popular engagements with the sources of information and entertainment of any era. For instance, Pauline Ripat (2006) discusses the role of the 'shadowy popular majority' as vital in sustaining Roman ideologies of Divination and thereby in creating our established understanding of Roman history. In Gustave le Bon's (1895/1996) late nineteenth century treatise on 'the crowd', which worried over the rise of populism and fascism at that time, he suggests that key moments of social change are largely brought by changes in the ideas of the people as much as any particular event. The media has of course played a significant role in determining and distributing ideas – the introduction of the printing press, the evolution of photography, the inception of cinema, broadcasting, the internet, data surveillance – have all intervened in the ways in which 'the people' come together and produce their broader understandings of the world. Even though we should not assume that these occur in universalising ways, reproducing normative 'stages' of progress, as we discussed in the last chapter (Shome, 2019).

Thinking of audiences as 'mobs' or 'crowds' betrays an uneven relationship between people in societies and this tends to be accompanied by ideas about social control. For instance, the word 'Mob' appeared in the English in the seventeenth century after the Restoration as an

34 ANCHOR

abbreviation of *mobile vulgus* or 'fickle populace' which presumed the lower classes, being less educated and sophisticated, to be easily swayed in their opinion (Butsch, 2008: 9). It also registered certain fears about the potential for unrest and unruly behaviour, since the lower classes do not have much invested in maintaining the current social order. The word mob therefore sets up a relationship whereby mobs are at once threatening to the social order and to be feared, at the same time as open to manipulation and to be controlled.

Butsch's accounts are largely referring to the rise of the 'mob' during processes of industrialising in the US where there are classed tensions through which the 'crowds' and 'workers' of the eighteenth and nineteenth centuries engaged in popular entertainment such as carnivals and theatre. Here, the lower classes could come together and were viewed by the ruling classes as dangerous in their unruly, active, engaged and even resistive engagements with culture (Stallybrass and White, 1986). As Richard Butsch (2008) articulates the 'taming' of audiences became part of the process of a civilising mission in the establishment of bourgeois society under the advances of industrialisation: 'Theatres become an integral part of the national confrontation between classes and their political values' (Butsch, 2000: 41).

Ways of seeing audiences, therefore, have often also been ways of articulating tensions *between* people and these are ultimately part of the social phenomena that are carried through, in different ways, from one epoch to another and to the present day. These histories, then, alert us to earlier conditions or 'anchors' that are valuable for us to still consider: First that the ways in which large groups of people act are often subject to concerns about social control and class tension and, second that in much earlier time periods 'activity' *and* 'interactivity' are characteristic of audience behaviour. Important for us to carry into our analysis of the present is the notion that 'audience sovereignty', that the audience held some power, existed in different ways long before it was heralded as a key characteristic of the internet era. We must therefore remember to circle-back and appreciate how audience struggles are located within broader evolving social tensions.

Such tensions around the rise of industrialisation and class antagonism have been central to ways of seeing audiences in critical academic thought. Early media studies thinking *began* as a concern with audiences, accounts of the 'mass media' audience rely on the theorisation of class struggles during the process of industrialisation. In the nineteenth century the shift from rural to urban cultures, the rise of factory work and mass production, and the collecting together of a large part of the populations' working and living arrangements in the newly developing cities of Europe and America, were met with the development of reproductive forms of art and broadcasting. This saw the evolution of the term 'mass' to describe audience, and consequently the development of the field of 'mass communications' within the academy. However, the European and American emphases upon the term 'mass' has a different inflection related to their different political stakes in their fears for the social contexts of the time. According to Paddy Scannell (2007) the different influences were related to the US associations with 'freedom' and the organisation of social life, whilst urban poverty in Europe became the key social concern for its intellectuals. This, put rather crudely, led to a distinction between two traditions for which the mass audience was of interest: the administrative (Functionalist) American tradition and the critical (Marxist) European Tradition, although Scannell (2007) is also at pains to point out that there were significant overlaps between the two.

The European tradition emerged from the Frankfurt School's Institute of Social Research which later found its home in the US after exile from Fascist Germany. The influence of the works of Theodor Adorno, Max Horkheimer, and Walter Benjamin in the 1930s possibly did not register so greatly at the time, as they have more recently to the still relatively new field of media studies.[3] This work is heavily influenced by the work of Karl Marx who in *Capital* elucidated a dominant theory of the relationship of 'the people' to capital. Marx described that in factory conditions, the worker must be alienated since he has no investment in the end-product and is enslaved by time through wage labour. This basic description from Marx serves as the important backdrop to understanding how ideas of the 'mass audience' were conceived in the tradition of the Frankfurt School.

Marx understands the capitalist conditions of existence based upon class antagonism and prescribed to a law of historical determinism meaning that antagonism must induce some revolutionary force. But since, and despite grave poverty, such universal revolutionary activity, (aside from in Russia) had not come about – and thus to some extent the

36 ANCHOR

Frankfurt School's theorisation of the mass audience began to explain why. Theodor Adorno and Max Horkheimer's (1944/1986) classic text the *Dialectic of Enlightenment* is a lament of capitalism's execution of the Enlightenment project whereby free thought and reason in the interests of a better moral society had been sacrificed for the pursuit of profit. For Marx and Engels (1848/1998) in *The Communist Manifesto*, they suggest that the ideas of the ruling elite also become the ideas of the ruled via their ownership of the means of production. This has therefore become a key spine for studying the media and audiences, since the media are responsible for the production and reproduction of ideas, making questions of interpretation and ideology central to audience research as we shall discuss more in Chapter 3. Using these ideas, Adorno and Horkheimer set to work on what they call the 'culture industry' – that is mass produced music, cinema, and radio – and suggest that it integrates its consumers from above.

It is in their main treatise on the culture industry that Adorno and Horkheimer forge their theoretical implications about the nature of the mass audience. They suggest that the mass audience is largely enchanted by the offerings of the mass media, distracted from the conditions of their existence and therefore unlikely to act in a radical or even reasonable fashion. Audience consumption of mass-produced products leads to increasing standardisation and lack of independent thought. The mass audience becomes interested in artificially manufactured art forms that are not part of a more authentic organic culture and thus become drawn into the culture of fantasy that pedals the ideals of capitalism. Thus, dangerously through amusements in leisure time, capitalism co-opts the free time of its workers, and in consuming the mass-produced fantasies of their labours, the 'mass audience' are only actually enhancing the interests of capital and profit rather than their own (see Chapter 5).

Whilst this decription has dominated a lot of thinking in Western media studies, the terms of 'mass' however have a different genealogy in other geographical contexts. For instance, Joe F. Khalil (2015) describes an insistence to understand the 'Arab world' as a 'mass' post 9/11, but calls for more nuanced and locally-sensitive understandings of the intersecting discourses of religious contexts. We can also see these ideas as having renewed resonance in a context where there is again a rising influence of far right thinking and populism across much of Europe and the US, and increasing concerns for the ways in which social media is reproducing social division (see Vaidhyanathan, 2018). Recall the discussion in Chapter 1 about how our online audience activity is captured, measured and 'nudged' in the extraction of capital by platform capitalism which presents new ways in which capital integrates our activities for its own ends. These ideas provide an important 'anchor' for ideas about audiences as workers that we will revisit in Chapter 5.

The fears for the audience, as it has been identified as a 'mass' and part of 'mass society' enveloped by mass-production as part of the growing sites of leisure and consumption take on a different characterisation to those earlier concerns of the 'mob'. Concerns about the 'mob' and 'crowd' were related to the masculinised fear of violent activity and the co-opting of public space. At the turn of the century as theatres looked to new markets they looked to incorporate women audiences with advances like the matinee which Butsch (2000) also points out coincides with the decline of audience sovereignty. Newly found freedoms for middle-class women and their growing engagement with consumer ideals about taste and lifestyle meant that women were also regular attendees at early cinema. Fears about the influence of cinema therefore were drawn around the idea of the vulnerable (female or child) spectator for whom the cinema apparatus was a deemed a far more potent psychological influence. If the 'mob' was largely characterised by masculine activity, the 'mass' is largely characterised as feminine passivity and the nature of developing societal concerns are reflected in this gendering (Huyssen, 1986).

In western contexts twentieth century social concerns were growing about women's new consumer freedoms and the kinds of messages 'filling their heads' from these evolving media forms. This assumes women to be passive dupes and it is against this backdrop that the important feminist audience work of the 1980s and 1990s took its cue. Their project started from the feminist position of valuing women's culture. For instance, Janice Radway (1984) explored the social and psychological reasons for women's consumption of romance fiction and Dorothy Hobson (1980) understood how radio and television offered an important social and structuring function for the housewife at home (Hobson, 1980). Purnima Mankekar's (1999) ethnography of affluent women television viewers in India discussed how popular texts allowed women to work through prevailing discourse of nationhood. Such work offered more contextualised and sociologically grounded research which sought to understand women's relationship to popular media against an earlier tide of pathologizing women's practices. These works were often sensitive to questions of emotion and pleasure which were instructive of gender relations in the social order, to which we will return (Chapter 4). This forms another important anchor for contemporary audience research, pressing us to think about everyday life and how feelings and sentiment are key to an evaluation of gendered contexts and inequalities.

If we want to understand the contemporary girl performing for TikTok then we need to draw on these histories. The feminist concerns of the 1980s and 1990s used audience research to interrogate women's apparent passive consumption of patriarchal fantasies and populated any over-easy account of womens' passivity with audience research which demonstrated women's consumption as a site of pleasure firmly located in gendered social contexts (for a more full account see Chapter 3). We might want to draw some parallels to now, as discussed in Chapter 1, in the context of a postfeminist media culture, where a whole host of feminist media studies shows us how feminism and neoliberalism has dovetailed so neatly that the appeals to young women about individual self-empowerment are potentially more divisive than liberatory.

Is the girl performing on TikTok with her consumer confidence entirely emblematic of this shift? We need to know how complete this neoliberal project is and to understand what are the 'warm bodies' doing on the ground, especially if our feminist project is to help resist the individualising impulses of postfeminist media culture. The pressures of postfeminist media culture apparently weigh heaviest on working-class women and black women who lack access to many of the resources for neoliberal success and in a context of widening social, racialised inequality (McRobbie, 2020). But empirical work on black girls on-line shows resistive experiences of community-building, creativity and joy (Jarmon, 2013; Sobande and Osei, 2020) which is in constant dialogue with online racist forms of oppression and abuse (Sobande, 2020). These are *lived* struggles and we need to continue to ask questions about how culture is invested in the digital spaces of the online world, where audiencing and performing become integrated phenomena and where online-offline experiences continually co-exist.

WAYS OF KNOWING AUDIENCES: CINEMA, RADIO, TV

As we have now seen, the struggle over classifying popular audiences is highly indicative of broader struggles between people, and each new popular entertainment form found itself at the centre of these struggles across different contexts. The rise of the 'mass media' is played out as part of the rapid period of seismic change brought by industrialisation which saw huge shifts in urban living, transport developments, and scientific advancement. At the same time, social relations were also changing: such as middle-class women starting to play a larger role in Anglo-American public life as a result of the Suffrage movement, and as part of the growth of leisure and consumption where women were emerging as educators in lifestyle, taste and cultivated living. Film exhibition was at the centre of these shifts. At first it toured theatres or appeared on the bill of live Vaudeville variety shows and were thus from the outset seen to appeal to the lower classes. Other spaces were shop-fronts, the 'Penny Gaffs' in the UK, whilst the first regular film screenings were in Nickelodeons in the US where store-fronts were converted in the motion picture show rooms. These spaces were thought to be part community-centre, part cinema. The precise make-up of the audiences of these emerging venues is still open to debate in film history (Sklar, 1990/2002), but cinema was a significant part of this new modern world and offered an important collective space for women and the lower classes to gather in significant ways. It is important to counter this with an understanding of its specificity. For instance, early accounts of cinema audiences in Calcutta were conjured through a different narrative, one that held to a sense of a 'viewing public' which needed to be educated in the context of de-colonisation and in an emerging democracy (Dass, 2015).

It is difficult to appreciate the wonderment of those early cinema audiences in seeing the moving image. Tom Gunning (1989) revisits the popular idea that audiences were terrified by the train coming towards them in their first encounter with Lumiere's '*Arrival of a train at a station*', as less about a naïve audience struggling with reality but more evidence of their astonishment at the cinema apparatus itself and the transformation to moving image. But this new apparatus which offered a mode of concentrated looking and spectacle engendered a new set of elite fears and patrician concerns over audiences. Children made up a large part of the cinema audience around the same time that a new regime of concerns around child protection, the banning of child labour and work in child psychology, was emerging.

Alongside the rapid increase in cinema-going through to the 1930s and the take-up of radio, came the first empirical research in order to generate knowledge about audiences in America. This consisted mostly of social-scientific ways of surveying audiences, concentrating not on the collective experience of inhabiting public space, but moreover on the individual psychological experience of watching films, such as numerous surveys on the concerns over the psychological 'effects' of movies on juvenile behaviour. Concerns arose about films having an overwhelming influence over vulnerable audiences where ideas and behaviours could be directly implanted into minds, meaning that audiences might lose control. Sociologist Herbert Blumer (1933), in the book *Movies and Conduct* describes juveniles' 'imitations' of films and characters and their 'emotional possession' by the intense conditions of the film experience.

Annette Kuhn (1988) describes how these concerns over early films' ability to induce physical effects such as sight problems or night terrors, formed part of the institutionalisation of child protection and the setting up of film censorship and classification boards. Many of these studies were commissioned by public bodies and represented strategic concerns as part of the 'administrative' tradition in American Communication Studies. The whole debate between whether the media have 'direct' effects upon audiences, also termed the 'hypodermic syringe theory' or the 'magic bullet theory', has been central to the formation of media and audiences research.

The arrival in the 1920s of broadcasting through early radio also generated new ways of knowing audiences. Early radio users in the US were known as 'fans' and the focus was largely on the technical apparatus and set-building in the early years. Audiences were DIY 'makers' of Crystal sets and transmitted messages to each other, more as 'wireless telegraphy'. Early listeners engaged in the complicated practice of getting a clear signal as the wonder of being able to 'listen' in your own home required a good deal of effort with the use of headsets making it initially a solitary and mostly male experience. (Moores, 1988). But as radio audiences grew rapidly over the 1920s and 1930s, and sets were manufactured in elaborate wooden cabinets so the domestic audience grew. No longer collected together in one place as in an auditorium or theatre but, audiences were dispersed, scattered across the nation in the privacy of their own homes and part of the changing conditions of suburbanisation that held people 'together' as they lived in more privatised family units (Silverstone, 1994).

Many of the fears engendered about the effects of the cinema transferred to radio. The move of the 'mass' audience from public space to domestic space contributed to this understanding of audiences as increasingly vulnerable, passive and potentially susceptible to messages and persuasion. This includes the now mythical idea that the broadcasting of HG Wells' *War of the Worlds* in 1938 on CBS induced 'mass' panic because listeners thought an invasion was real (Cantril and Allport, 1935). This event fuelled Cantril's (1940) research into understanding the role of mass broadcasting in inciting a mass response which suggested that some audiences who lacked a 'critical ability' were more likely to be over-whelmed than others, and this contributed to a research agenda worried about mass influence and persuasion. Again, Cantrils' suggestion about 'critical ability' was charged towards those with lower education and class, assuming that what was needed was better media education for the 'masses'. Concerns over 'mass persuasion' have often resurfaced, fuelled by increasing concerns over the power of radio as a tool for education and propaganda, particularly during wartime (Katz, 1987; Mattelart, 2000).

But we must understand these as prescient concerns which can offer anchors to our current thinking. Questions of mass persuasion are resurfacing again in the current debates about the influence of 'fake news' and 'misinformation' as it has developed across social networking sites (SNS), which has circumvented more institutionalised forms of news gathering. There is a concern about the scale of fake news and that heavy internet users are more susceptible to misinformation which is ultimately undermining democracy (Glaser, 2017). But, as is repeated from histories of research into audience behaviour, sweeping assumptions about audiences are rarely born out completely when audience research is conducted on the ground. Nelson and Taneja (2018) in their research on online audience behaviour in the run up to the 2016 US Presidential election, suggest some caution showing that the fake news audience is still a relatively small and disloyal group of heavy users who will also be more likely to encounter other forms

42 ANCHOR

of news consumption. What this shows though is that many of the models around audience behaviour recirculate, and that it is important to be cautious about blanket observations about audience behaviour and to circle-back to understand how and why certain observations about audiences take hold around particular social concerns at particular moments in time.

This kind of revisionism has allowed a more contemporary audience researcher like David Morley (1992) to revisit Paul Merton's (1946) work on 'mass persuasion' arguing for its more sophisticated sociological-grounding in explaining just how persuasion is different to propaganda. Paddy Scannell argues that Lazarsfeld and Merton's ([1948] 2004) later essay contains the same traces as many of the ideas that resurfaced in the 1970s and 80s to form the 'newly-quilted media studies' of the British tradition. Lazarsfeld and Merton's discussion of the establishment of 'pseudo-relationships' in persuasion has been a resurfacing concern to research on media audiences and again can 'anchor' some of our contemporary theorising. Whilst psychologists Horton and Wohl (1956) pointed out the way broadcasting and its personalities work to establish a 'para-social' relationship with audiences, I have shown in my own empirical research with audiences how those relationships translate to everyday interactions at home, especially with genres like television talk shows and magazine shows (Wood, 2009). My research though made some connections between how that conversational invitation is embedded within the self-reflexive cultures of the 2000s in the making of modern, gendered and classed identities.

These same issues have moved through broadcasting into the current digital landscape, in the developing attachments that audiences have with celebrities, in the ways in which social media encourages a series of relationships based on likes and comments and with the growing number of bloggers and influencers. A whole host of marketing and advertising research into audiences is concerned with assessing and measuring how influencers build their brands and attract 'followers' (e.g. Taillon et al., 2020; Lou. 2021) or the ways in which influencers might affect public opinion in the field of public relations (Abidin, 2015; Dhanesh and Duthler, 2019). In this environment, the terms of 'distanced-friendships' set in motion by earlier forms of broadcast media are of course evolving and those earlier phrases like 'pseudo' and 'para' to describe mediated relationships barely seem to capture the way in which social media relationships have become a central feature of the digital circuits of commercial culture. It is important that we understand where these new relationships come from, having precedents in much older 'mass' audience engagements as we circle back to attempt to trace the relationships with social change.

Quite often in accounts of media effects tradition(s), simple models of communication are induced, such as that of sender-message-receiver which presumes a linear and direct pattern of media effects and produces those descriptions such as the 'hypodermic syringe' model or 'bullet theory'. As we have seen, notions of effects have moved through different phases, from the dominant effects of the early propaganda models, to the limited effects of later social science research, back to the dominant effects largely of television through an emphasis upon psychology. In each shift, the audience is presumed to be a vulnerable and gullible mass that needs protecting and television is seen to have a dominant effect above other social influences. On these grounds contemporary media and audience studies has often rejected the effects tradition but according to Livingstone (1996) this is largely due to a stereotyped account of media effects which is usually scapegoated by the Bandura et al (1961) 'Bobo Doll' experiment. Mostly, the research on direct media effects has been inconclusive and remains unresolved, partly because the debate is about the limits of social science research, rather than any concern with the media in particular.

Nevertheless is it worth pointing out that debates about media effects do not go away and re-emerge in popular consciousness through media panics. Causal links are often inferred at particular moments of crisis; when society (or the media) are at a loss as to explain particular abhorrent social behaviour it is easy to find blame within the media. Research in psychology continues to suggest that exposure to violence, for instance in video games, might have a de-sensitising and anti-social effect on young people (e.g. Fraser et al., 2012).

The debate about effects has continued and mutated in research with audiences. This is partly why we continue to need good quality research on media influence, despite the difficulties and problematics associated with social-scientific research on generalisable patterns of social behaviour that have largely assumed vulnerable and passive victims of media influence. Research by Aeron Davis (2006) for

44 ANCHOR

instance, has shown how elite 'rational' fund managers at the London Stock Exchange also succumb to collective pressures of media influence in the context of trading cultures. Therefore, it would be simply wrong to assume that the media have no effect because it is difficult to find, but it is equally wrong to assume that the media have isolated determinate effects simply because we want to look for them. For a good discussion in what is at stake in these positions between the determining assumptions of the older effects tradition and what we might miss by dismissing effects completely see Barker and Petley (2001). This more complex picture broadly supports my wider argument for an emphasis upon what is *social and cultural* about the relationships between the media and audiences – as complexly embroiled within wider social relations *between* people.

THE HISTORICAL AUDIENCE: MEMORY, DETECTIVE WORK AND REVISIONISM

As we have seen, audiences are brought into view at particular moments to help explain important key aspects of social change – and we have at our disposal a range of ways of 'seeing' and 'knowing' audiences from the vantage point of particular social problems and the emergence of academic audience research in different traditions. We can see that key concerns emerge which have continued relevance for the contemporary mediated environment, some of which are centred around the arrival of particular new technologies and/or key moments of social upheaval. The history of audience research is therefore complexly responsive to, and interwoven within, social and political shifts.

From these histories, we can see the importance of gathering evidence 'from the ground'. Recall Sonia Livingstone's (2019) account in chapter one of the way in which the 'grand narratives' of media studies often serve to eclipse any sense of audience experiences, assuming as they do a set of aggregated individuals swept by the tide of technological change. Jerome Bourdon (2015), in a similar fashion appeals for the 'detextualisation' of historical audiences, to move away from an understanding of audiences at the level of grand narratives based on 'axiologies of hopes and fears' (2015: 8 citing Altick, 1998: 370–371). Audience histories are vital to providing the contextual narratives and counter-narratives of any settled accounts of media history. These can only work to give us more precise tools of analysis with which to analyse social change, which is surely why we do Media and Cultural Studies at all.

How to do this as audience historians is difficult though, since we rely on what is accessible and 'lying around' as historical evidence. Bourdon (2015) helpfully gives us a typology of approaches, from above, from the side and from below

> We will start with sources 'from above' (texts emanating from the professional actors who produced media messages or the political actors who supervise them), move to sources 'from the side' (texts provided not by the elites from above, but various witnesses of the audience of their time, journalists, writers, etc.) and continue with sources 'from below' (through self-reports of audiences, testimonies at the time, including in diaries or – for future historians – comments on a programme on Facebook).
>
> (2015: 12)

There are many more accounts of media history 'from above' because of the availability of institutional histories, but assumptions about audiences are often derived from what professionals and institutions wanted to know about them – often statistical analysis for political or commercial ends. This evidence is important but must be accompanied by other available sources – from the side or from below – journalistic accounts, texts of the time, popular writing, advertising and in the spaces where we might find the voices of the time——for instance in the Mass Observation Archives, described at the outset of this chapter.

One of the main ways that we might be able to trace social change is of course through existing generations and through their media experiences which is a method that is time-limited and urgent. It is easy to forget, as we look at the sophistication of contemporary youth audiences and 'digital natives' just how much media and social change older audiences have lived through in the last century (Harrington, Bielby, and Bardo, 2014). Jackie Stacey's (1994) work *Star Gazing* used letters and questionnaires to access the voices of women fans of film stars of the 1940s and 1950s – importantly centring ideas about women's audiences, consumption and desire, again influenced by

46 ANCHOR

a feminist project to value women's culture. This was an important move in film studies – which had not at that point really ever been interested in the film viewer as a real person but only as a potential spectator, conjured through the apparatus of the film text.

Annette Kuhn's (2002) text *An Everyday Magic* researched the golden-age of cinema of the 1930s and complemented the accounts of film advertising, reviews and cinema in popular culture with the voices of hundreds of cinema-goers who were enchanted by the cinema at the time through oral history interviews. Against the theoretical analyses of the film spectator and the statistical accounts of high box office audience figures, Kuhn charts how going to the cinema was part of social accounts of neighbourhood daily life, social rhythms and relationships as much as it was about the films themselves. Cinema was a vital space for 'girl talk' and its affordability offered working-class audiences access to world they could not have otherwise known. For these audiences the attachments to the cinema, nurtured in youth, lived with them through life: 'For this movie-mad generation, the dreams were saturated with cinema; today 'their' cinema is gone. But the dreams are not forgotten' (2002: 134) Similarly, some recent research I have conducted with Stuart Hanson on older viewers' memories of particular local cinemas shows how for audiences the local cinema is a nostalgic site of comfort and care (Hanson and Wood, 2021).

Scholars of television audiences have documented how the domestication of the technology evokes audience memories as the technology and the form becomes ensconced in the fabric of the everyday and the familial. Memories of television programmes come to life through recalling family occasions and experiences (O'Sullivan, 1997; Collie, 2013). Hazel Collie's (2013) interviews with women viewers of different generations shows how important and significant those gendered emotional attachments are – pushing back against theoretical ideas about television as an 'amnesiac' medium because so much of its form and organisation is about the narrating of the present. While it is of course important to note, as many do, that memories are unreliable constructions of the 'truth' of any situation, the importance here is not so much the accuracy of these memories but the way the testimonies of audiences drawn out in the research assert television's significance within everyday life (Dhoest, 2015). These types of narratives are important for how they flesh out the assumptions of media statistics and sweeping theoretical accounts of the social influence of particular media forms. They contribute to our understandings of the way in which media audiences are involved in memory work and in collective accounts of the media's role in the creation of cultural memory and in social change (O'Sullivan and Wood, 2017). These are questions that also take on new potency in the digital era as the digital provides extensive archives for the generation of new forms of mediated memory. (see Neiger et al., 2011; De Kosnik, 2016).

Historical work tracing audiences therefore offers us space to revise settled ideas and accounts about the media and social change. Susan Douglas (2004) offers us what she calls an 'archaeology of radio listening from the 1920s to the present' drawing on the available knowledge, listings and archives and the radio programs themselves, of which relatively little remains because much radio was not recorded. Douglas highlights American radio's generation of relatively heterogeneous audiences that were interactive and often reactionary characterised by what she refers to as 'technological insurgency' since many developments in early radio came from audiences themselves. What is important is that while now radio may seem relatively low-tech and unglamorous, especially when faced by the complexity and potential of digital services, its narratives of development sometimes confound what we might have assumed about its audiences.

Douglas directly pulls into view Sherry Turkle's (1996) work in *Life on the Screen* where she first suggests that virtual life and the internet help to multiply our sense of identity by virtue of the alternative worlds we can occupy and the multiple personas we can generate. This had become a relatively settled idea of the way in which the internet has accelerated postmodern ideas about the fracturing of identity and Turkle herself has shifted from her more positive account of this shift as we saw in Chapter 1. But in circling back, Douglas suggests that such a narrative of radio might also have been constructed:

> Radio, by cultivating different modes of listening, also fostered people's tendency to feel fragmented into many selves which were called forth in rapid succession or sometimes all at the same time.

(2004: 9)

48 ANCHOR

As I have pointed out, earlier media forms clearly play a part in preparing the ground for evolving audience engagements, which whilst audience historians seek to make these connections, those espousing the radical potential of new technology, sometimes rarely do. In the pressure to look forward, we sometimes forget to 'circle back'.

In my historical audience research described at the beginning of this chapter, I wanted to look more closely at the readily settled account of the feminisation of television viewer. Lynn Spigel's (1992) central historical work *Make Room for TV* describes the way in which American television established itself through advertising and press narratives with its primary address to 'Mrs daytime consumer'. In the UK Janet Thumim's (2004) work, using the BBC archives and accounts of programming drew out similar parallels. The take-up of television as a technology amid the consumer boom of the 1950s and the discursive rhetoric of the 'modern home' led to an established account of the close relationship of television to the figure of 'the housewife'. Whilst these are both excellent histories what troubled me, especially as a feminist, was the absence of the voice of 'the housewife'. She is both ever-present – conjured in advertising, in institutional accounts of the desired viewer at home, in the direct address of the television programmes – but rather silent in her own account of this new technology that has been characterised so readily as *for* her. What did she think? What did she have to say? I was curious as to whether more voices could be found and so I turned to what was 'lying around' and to the archives of the Mass Observation Study which have proved to be fruitful sources for historians of cinema, and to a lesser extent, television (O'Sullivan, 1997; Ornebring, 2007).

The Mass Observation Study was admittedly a very particular, and perhaps peculiar, set of studies originally conducted by Charles Madge, Humphrey Jennings and Tom Harrisson who drew together a large of panel of observers, diarists and commentators to document a 'science of ourselves' in order to detail 'ordinary life' between 1937 and 1949, continuing later as market research.[4] One of their directives, conducted in 1949 directly surveyed 'ordinary people's' opinions of the coming of television, and in these responses were the voices of women, many of whom described themselves as housewives. What I found there was a good deal of resistance to television, especially as the poor quality of the screen would operate as an unwelcome

ANCHOR 49

distraction to the women's roles in the home and they were concerned about their time for household chores. Lynn Spigel's (1992) point about the tension between home as a site of leisure and of work for housewives proves to be a key issue in the MO Directive. This finding needs to be put into the social context of many working-class women finding new pride as housewives, away from household service jobs, and in the development of new post-war housing projects where they became homeowners in their own right. I also found that there were more negotiated positions around the suburban domestication of entertainment and other consumer desires to get dressed up and go out – than we can find in many of the accepted histories, as well as preferences for genre that have often been assumed as masculine. Indeed, television 'may not have been easily accepted by women as a key symbol of the modern home or as the ideal site for mass entertainment as it might be assumed, and television was not always the housewife's choice at all' (Wood, 2015: 13).[5]

Whilst this was a small survey, its very existence as an alternative narrative is important to our overall assumptions about the role of television in social change. Women's role as pioneer audiences of television needed to be negotiated in relation to the changing roles of women at the time. As I opened this discussion in this chapter, with archival work on media audiences, I cannot now see how millennial girls approach TikTok as *their* public culture without imagining 'housewife aged 18' contemplating television. How different the challenges to their relationship between public and private worlds, how differently hinged they are to domestic life as labour, and how similarly attached they are to 'getting it (gender) right'. Picking up the voices of the past wherever we can, therefore, is an important endeavour: It helps us to test and trouble accepted histories, but it also helps us anchor assumptions about change and show us more precisely the distance travelled between then and now.

CONCLUSION

I opened this chapter with the question: *How can audience histories, help us to understand social change?* The history of audience research is a history of repetition and the recycling of social patterns and social relations within which media forms are both situated and generative, but it is *not* a linear narrative of change and progress. Many of these histories have brought audiences into view in particular ways of seeing and knowing audiences, fearful for what 'the people' might do once collected together in any particular way. The ways of 'knowing' audiences tell us a great deal about their resonance with shifting social tensions, particularly in Anglo-American histories in relation to class and gender. Many of the pejorative ways in which audiences have been determined as 'mobs' or 'passive dupes', tell us a good deal about the social relations of power and social control, particularly as they are connected to key moments of social change or emancipation and as they are located in different geographical contexts.

Whilst of course we still only have a partial history of the development of audiences, the important narrative that I have tried to hold on to is that all audiences' histories are the histories of the media's role in social relations. Many of the same tensions get recycled, and it is important for us to 'circle-back' and remember some of the implications from older research as we try to map the present. I have tried where possible to alert the reader to some key 'anchors' – precedents of ideas that are still so very useful for about thinking about precise nature and character of the contemporary digital landscape. I hope this process encourages the reader to think of the many more than I have had space to set out here, but some of these include ideas about labour, audience sovereignty and the pseudo-relationships of influencing. Whilst we have largely rejected some of the original terms of the 'effects' debate, we are still bound to ask questions which try to think about how media is central to the winds of social change and to the broader ways in which people understand the world around them.

If we think of 'audiencing' as set out in Chapter 1 as a way of seeing the nature of the audience as productive of social formations, then we should also use our means for conducting historical audience research to grasp some of the contextual specificity that fleshes out the broader sweeping grand narratives or expectations of social change. We can use revisionism to know more about the past and also to decolonise our understanding of it – attempting to usurp the tendency to see the Global South from the vantage point of the global north (Willems, 2014) because it is important to counter some of these normative assumptions with alternative histories. This project of historical audience research suggests that it is important to historicise and 'anchor' the present media context within older legacies and trajectories. We must also conduct audience histories that give us space for revision as we remember that our understanding of an audience is not done because media technology has moved on. Thus far, I have tried to do this with only passing reference to many of the dominant traditions of 'active audiences' as they have come through Cultural Studies and Communication Studies, but I will turn to these important legacies in the next chapter.

NOTES

1 The Mass Observation Archive specialises in material about everyday life in Britain. It contains papers generated by the original Mass Observation social research organisation (1937 to early 1950s), and newer material collected continuously since 1981 (Mass Observation Project). http://www.massobs.org.uk/

2 You can see examples of these accounts on the BBC website https://www.bbc.com/historyofthebbc/100-voices/birth-of-tv/watching-at-home/

3 This is because many were not translated into English until the 1970s by the *New Left Review*.

4 Its social research has been described as more of a left-ish quasi-political social movement and the make-up of participants less 'ordinary' than they had originally hoped.

5 In subsequent work, the directives which asked about the arrival of commercial television (ITV) in 1955 offered a similar story where there was much more friction from women reiterating class-based concerns about the dumbing-down of culture than the idealised image of the housewife-consumer portrays. In keeping with historical revisions of the notion of the 'housewife-citizen' (Zweiniger-Bargielowska, 1994) there was an articulation of concerns in keeping with public and political debate (Wood and Kay, 2021).

REFERENCES

Abidin, C. (2015) 'Communicative Intimacies: Influencers and Perceived Interconnectedness', *Ada: A Journal of Gender, New Media, & Technology* 8. 1–16.

Adorno, T. and Horkheimer, M. ([1944] 1986) *Dialectic of Enlightenment*. London: Verso.

Bandura, A., Ross, D., and Ross, S.A. (1961) 'Transmission of aggression through imitation of aggressive models', *Journal of Abnormal and Social Psychology* 63 (3): 575–582.

Barker, M. and Petley, J. (2001) *Ill Effects* (Communication and Society). London: Taylor & Francis Group.

Blumler, H. (1933) *Movies and Conduct*. New York: Macmillan.

ANCHOR

Bourdon, J. (2015) 'Detextualisation: How to do a history of audiences', *European Journal of Communication Studies* 30 (1): 7–21.

Butsch, R. (2000) *The Making of American Audiences: From Stage to Television 1750-1990*. Cambridge: Cambridge University Press.

Butsch, R. (2008) *The Citizen Audience: Crowds, Publics and Individuals*. London: Routledge.

Butsche, R. and Livingstone, S. (2015) 'Introduction: "Translating audiences, provincializing Europe"', in Butsche, R. and Livingstone, S. (eds.) *Meaning of Audiences: Comparative Discourses*. London and New York: Routledge.

Cantril, H. (1940) *The Invasion from Mars: A Study in the Psychology of Panic*. Princeton, NJ: Princeton University Press.

Cantril, H. and Allport, G. (1935) *The Psychology of Radio*. New York: New York Harper.

Collie, H. (2013) '"It's just so hard to bring it to mind": The significance of 'wallpaper' in the gendering of television memory work', *VIEW Journal of European Television History and Culture* 2 (3): 13–21.

Dass, M. (2015) 'A consuming public: Movie audiences in the Bengali cultural imaginary', in Butsche, R. and Livingstone, S. (eds.) *Meaning of Audiences: Comparative Discourses*. London and New York: Routledge, pp 97–110.

Davis, A. (2006) 'Media effects and the question of the rational audience: Lessons from the financial markets', *Media, Culture & Society* 28 (4): 603–625.

De Kosnik, A. (2016) *Rogue Archives: Digital Cultural Memory and Media Fandom*. Cambridge, MA: MIT Press.

Dhanesh, G.S. and Duthler, G. (2019) 'Relationship management through social media influencers: Effects of followers' awareness of paid endorsement', *Public Relations Review* 45 (3): 101765.

Dhoest, A. (2015) 'Audience retrospection as a source of historiography: Oral history interviews on early television experiences', *European Journal of Communication* (London) 30 (1): 64–78.

Douglas, S. J. (2004) *Listening In: Radio and the American Imagination*. Minneapolis: University of Minnesota Press.

Fraser, A. M., et al. (2012) 'Associations between violent video gaming, empathic concern, and prosocial behavior toward strangers, friends, and family members', *Journal of Youth and Adolescence* 41 (5): 636–649.

Glaser, A. (2017) 'Apple CEO Tim Cook says fake news is "killing people's minds" and tech needs to launch a counterattack', Recode, February 12. Available at: https://www.vox.com/2017/2/12/14591522/apple-ceo-tim-cook-tech-launch-campaign-fake-news-fact-check (accessed 3/10/23).

Gunning, T. (1989) 'An aesthetics of astonishment: Early film and the (in) credulous spectator', *Art and Text* 34: 31–45.

Hanson, S. and Wood, H. (2021) 'The cinema, the town and 'my films': generating memory-scapes of local cinema-going' HoMER (History of Movie-going, Exhibition and Reception) annual conference University of Maynooth online.

Harrington, C.L., Bielby, D., and Bardo, A. (eds.). (2014) *Ageing, Media and Culture*. Lanham, MD: Lexington Books.

Hartley, J. (1992) *Tele-ology: Studies in Television*. London: Routledge.

ANCHOR 53

Hobson, D. (1980) 'Housewives and the mass media', in Hall, S., et al. (eds.) *Culture, Media, Language* London: Hutchinson, pp. 104–114.

Horton, D. and Wohl, R. (1956) 'Mass communication as para-social interaction: Observations on intimacy at a distance', *Psychiatry* 19 (3): 215–229.

Huyssen, A. (1986) 'Mass culture as woman: Modernism's other', in Modleski, T. and Woodward, K. (eds.) *Studies in Entertainment.* Bloomington, IN: Indiana University Press, pp. 188–207.

Jarmon, R. (2013) *Black Girls are From the Future: Essays on Race, Digital Creativity and Pop Culture.* Washington, DC: Jarmon Media.

Kennedy, M. (2020) "'If the rise of the TikTok dance and e-girl aesthetic has taught us anything, it's that teenage girls rule the internet right now': TikTok celebrity, girls and the Coronavirus crisis', *European Journal of Cultural Studies*, 23(6): 1069–1076. https://doi.org/10.1177/1367549420945341

Khalili, J.F. (2015) "'The mass wants this!": How politics, religion and media industries shape discourses about audiences in the Arab world', in Butsche, R. and Livingstone, S. (eds.) *Meaning of Audiences: Comparative Discourses.* London and New York: Routledge, pp. 111–122.

Kuhn, A. (1988) *Cinema, Censorship and Sexuality 1909-1925.* London: Routledge.

Annette Kuhn (2002) *An Everyday Magic, Cinema and Cultural Memory.* London and New York: I.b. Tauris.

Lazarsfeld, P. and Merton, R. ([1948] 2004) 'Mass communication, popular taste and organised social action', in Peters, J.D. and Simonson, P. (eds.) *Mass Communication and American Social Thought.* Lanham, MD: Rowman and Littlefield, pp. 230–241.

Le Bon, G. (1995) The crowd. New Brunswick, N.J.: Transaction Pub.

Livingstone, S. (1996) 'On the continuing problems of media effects research', in Curran, J. and Gurevitch, M. (eds.) *Mass Media and Society* (2nd ed.). London: Edward Arnold, pp. 305–324.

Livingstone, S. (2019) 'Audiences in an age of datafication: Critical questions of media research', *Television and New Media* 20 (2): 170–183.

Lou, C. (2021) 'Social media influencers and followers: Theorization of a trans-parasocial relation and explication of its implications for influencer advertising', *Journal of Advertising* 51 (1): 4–21.

Marx, K. and Engels, F. (1848/1998) *The Communist Manifesto: A Modern Edition.* New edn. London: Verso.

Mankekar, P. (1999) *Screening Culture, Viewing Politics: An Ethnography of Television, Womanhood, and Nation in Postcolonial India.* Durham, NC: Duke University Press.

Mattelart, A. (2000) *Networking the World 1794-2000* (trans. L. Carey-Libbrecht and J.A. Cohen) Minneapolis, MN and London: University of Minnesota Press.

McRobbie, A. (2020) *Feminism and the Politics of Resilience: Essays on Gender, Media and the End of Welfare.* Cambridge: Polity Press.

Merton, R. (1946) *Mass Persuasion.* New York: Free Press.

Moores, S. (1988) "'The box on the dresser": Memories of early radio and everyday life', *Media, Culture and Society* 12 (1): 23–40.

ANCHOR

Morley, D. (1992) *Television, Audiences, and Cultural Studies*. London and New York: Routledge.

Neiger, M., Zandberg, E., and Meyers, O. (2011). *On Media Memory: Collective Memory in a New Media Age*. London, Palgrave.

Nelson, J.L. and Taneja, H. (2018) 'The small, disloyal fake news audience: The role of audience availability in fake news consumption', *New Media & Society* 20 (10): 3720–3737.

Ornebring, H. (2007) 'Writing the history of television audiences: The coronation and the mass observation archive', in Wheatley, H. (ed.) *Re-viewing Television History: Critical Issues in Television Historiography*. London: IB Tauris, pp. 170–183.

O'Sullivan, T. (1997) 'Television memories and cultures of viewing 1950-65', in Corner, J. (eds.) *Popular Television in Britain: Studies in Cultural History*, London: BFI, p. 163.

O'Sullivan, T. and Wood, H. (2017) 'Space and place to remember: Television in the National Space Centre', in Kay, J.B., Mahoney, C. Meakin, C. and Shaw, C. (2016) *Mediated Pasts: Memory and Visual Culture*. Jefferson: McFarland 220–240.

Ripat, P. (2006) 'Roman Omens, Roman Audiences and Roman History', *Greece and Rome* 53 (2): 155–174.

Scannell, P. (2007) *Media and Communication*. London and New York: Sage.

Shome, R. (2019) 'When Postcolonial studies interrupts media studies', *Communication, Culture and Critique* 12: 305–322.

Sklar, R. (2002) [1990]. *Film: An International History of the Medium* (2nd ed.). Prentice Hall. New Jersey.

Silverstone, R. (1994) *Television and Everyday Life*. London: Routledge.

Sobande, F. (2020) *The Digital Lives of Black Women in Britain*. London: Palgrave.

Sobande, F. and Osei, K. (2020) 'An African City: Black women's creativity, pleasure, diasporic (dis) connections and resistance through aesthetic media practices and scholarship', *Communication, Culture & Critique* 13 (2): 204–221.

Spigel, L. (1992) *Make Room for TV: Television and the Family Ideal in Post-War America*. Chicago, IL: Chicago University Press.

Stacey, J. (1994) *Star Gazing: Hollywood Cinema and Female Spectatorship*. New York: Routledge.

Stallybrass, P. and White, A. (1986) *The Politics and Poetics of Transgression*. London: Methuen.

Taillon, B., et al. (2020) 'Understanding the relationships between social media influencers and their followers: The moderating role of closeness'," *The Journal of Product & Brand Management* 29 (6): 767–782.

Thumim, J. (2004) *Inventing Television Culture*. Oxford: Oxford University Press.

Vaidhyanathan, S. (2018) *Anti-social Media: How Facebook Disconnects Us and Undermines Democracy*. Oxford: Oxford University Press.

Turkle, S. (1996) *Life on the Screen: Identity in the Age of the Internet New York*. Simon & Schuster.

Willems, W. (2014) 'Beyond normative de-westernisation: Examining media culture from the vantage point of the Global', *The Global South* 8 (1): 7–23.

Williams, R. (1974) *Television: Technology and Cultural Form*. London: Fontana.

Wood, H. (2009) *Talking with Television: Women, Television and Modern self-reflexivity.* Urbana, IL: Illinois University Press.

Wood, H. (2015) 'Television—the housewife's choice? The 1949 mass observation television directive, reluctance and revision', *Media History* 21 (3): 342–359. https://doi.org/10.1080/13688804.2015.1015512

Wood, H. and Kay, J.B. (2021) '"I am against Americanizing England. Ordinary TV does not seem to have an elevating influence": Class, gender, public anxiety, and the responses to the arrival of commercial television in the mass observation archive, UK', *Feminist Media Studies* 21 (4): 523–538.

Zweiniger-Bargielowska, I. (1994) 'Rationing, austerity and the conservative party recovery after 1945', *Historical Journal* 37 (1): 173–197.

3

MEAN

SCENARIO: GOGGLEBOX (CHANNEL 4 2013–PRESENT)

Gogglebox (Channel 4 2013–) is a long-running popular television pro-gramme broadcast on Channel 4 in the UK. It has cemented itself as a popular staple of British television by simply recording the laughs, cries, joys and despair of 'ordinary' audiences watching their televi-sion sets in the comfort of their own homes. In many ways this feels like a nostalgic programme since it at once records diverse house-hold units around a singular set in the living room of the kind we hear is being substituted, if not eclipsed, in the personalised media environment of streaming on-demand. It also records these diverse (by race, class and sexual orientation) audiences' reactions to the same key programmes of the moment – the most popular dramas, news segments, documentaries and light entertainment shows, conjuring a kind of 'national family' just as we try to grasp a picture of the more fragmented niche audiences across the digital landscape.

I often use a scene from Gogglebox in my teaching on television audiences. In particular, it is a scene where the Gogglebox viewers are watching an episode of Educating Yorkshire (Channel 4) – a

DOI: 10.4324/9781003414575-4

MEAN 57

factual programme about teachers and pupils in a Northern school. In the episode an English teacher handles a boy's stammer by asking him to read a poem whilst listening to music and there is an incredibly moving moment when the boy, who previously struggled with his speech, enunciates clearly as though his stammer has disappeared. The boy is elated, the teacher is thrilled, the Gogglebox audiences on the programme cry across their variously arranged living rooms which are all still oriented around the television set, whilst they discuss the situation and their related experiences. And my students also tear-up in the classroom.

I use the example of Gogglebox here, not just to illuminate the very emotional relationships that audiences have with media forms, which we will come to in the next chapter, but because it is helpful in understanding how audiences make-meaning in multiple ways. Most obvious might be the persistence of traditional, linear, collective viewing habits which help to produce social, familial and national conversation, even in the face of alternative modes of consumption. But it is also helpful because it articulates something of the way in which audiences make texts meaningful as they view, precisely in the locations of their viewing. Texts have a social life through which they become meaningful in their interactions with audiences, they do not 'mean' alone and it has long been the project of audience research informed by Cultural Studies to grasp the complex relations between media texts and social life in ethnographic contexts.

However, interrogating questions of meaning-making, since the arrival of the internet has been relatively scattered and approached often without the lens of audience studies. This is mainly for reasons outlined in the first chapter in terms of the more complex boundaries around what we identify as 'texts' or 'audiences' in the participatory framework offered up by digital media. In the example above, this moment of television is described for YouTube as, 'Mustaraf overcomes his stammer' and it has over 200,000 views from just one of the many reposts. The dispersal of texts across platforms of course means that audiences also share, like, comment upon, remake and create new meanings for their own consumption and distribution, enhancing the meaning of the original text. Texts take on alternative formations as they can be put to use by audience engagement across digital platforms. The comments below the re-posting of this clip of Musharaf include things like, 'still one of the most inspirational bits of TV I've seen', 'I'm in tears watching this', 'greatest moment in British TV history' with testimonies from viewers about their experiences with stammering, their relationships with teachers, or a variety of comments on social issues such as the condition of the teaching profession, or social understandings of invisible disabilities. The conditions for 'making' meaning therefore become multiplied and varied embedded across multiple moments, spaces, communicative contexts and their lived experiences that are also particular to a set of circumstances in the British conjunctural moment.

Let us just unpick from this example some of the various frames for meaning-making that we see coming together. We can see the way in which the text takes on meaning as a 'ritual' form of communication and used in the everyday fabric of social life in the ways they form part of the social relations in all of these alternative familial groups. We can also see evidence of 'transmission' forms of communication - that is the transference of ideas or 'messages' here about the qualities and experience of teaching and learning in a Northern school. Such a distinction between 'ritual' and 'transmission' forms of communication was originally posed by James Carey in 1989 and had tended to be researched as separate and distinct entities. However, it is obvious from this example that these forms are being mutually produced through the ways in which texts take on life in their immediate social contexts. These then can take on other forms in the interpersonal exchanges encouraged by the commenting on YouTube or perhaps in the use of 'second-screens' as people tweet and extend their living-room conversations. The varied and extended ways in which audiences then engage in a series of digital practices through a variety of different forms to make meaning in the current conjuncture, denotes how interpersonal and mediated communication are much more closely and ritually imbricated, and this demands that we try to hold these elements together in our research by interrogating over-lapping processes of meaning-making.

QUESTION: HOW SHOULD THE RESEARCHER APPROACH THE OVERLAPPING PROCESSES OF MEANING-MAKING?

Legacies of media audience research can prepare us for this question at hand, but we should remember that audience research, as it was posed at the heart of the twentieth century, was often concerned with whether audiences were 'active' rather than 'passive' receptors of media. This is a question which seems so oversimplified now in a context where being 'active' users does not necessarily equate to any politically resistive potential, but rather to the platforms through which we regularly and ritually engage and are ultimately *inter*-active. In this chapter, I want to remind the contemporary media researcher of two key legacies around the 'active audience' which focussed upon questions of media 'use' – the 'uses and gratifications' tradition – and questions of 'meaning' – from Cultural Studies – both of which can be rearticulated for the complexity of the current conjuncture. The first emerged in the administrative tradition largely in US communications theory, in what was described as the 'uses and gratifications' model and the second grew from Cultural Studies' audience research which was influenced by a Gramscian position that hoped that the space for political negotiation might live in the reception practices of audiences. Here, unusually, I want to draw out these two positions, which have been largely separated out in the field of media studies, and put them in conversation with each other in order to further deal with the current complexities of 'audiencing' as made visible through *Gogglebox* and its extension intodigital into digital practices.

As outlined in Chapter 2, early mass communication theory generated one of the key dualisms of the field which centred around the debate between active versus passive audiences. The audiences of propaganda driven by an administrative 'Effects' theory were largely thought of as passive, duped by political ends or as in the case of the Frankfurt School, were positioned as 'masses' deceived by the commercial appeal of the new cultural industries. We might want to draw some parallels here with the ways in which, under the analyses of data capitalism, our submission to surveillance regimes of data extraction

60 MEAN

position audiences as agentless entities in similar ways. The primers left to us by the Frankfurt School could easily describe how we are now blindly playing along with capitalism as we hyper-consume and interact online whilst delivering our data for further commodification and profit elsewhere (Zuboff, 2019). All the time, arguably, audiences are being ideologically tricked by feelings of 'choice' and 'control' whilst at the same time being given no choice about access to our own data and privacy. We will return to this discussion in Chapter 5 about work, but for now it is important to note that these kind of assumptions do not help us to grasp the complexity of the way in which audience members live with media in their daily lives – or of the ways in which such potential forms of 'passivity' sit next to the potential for connection and collaboration, 'activity', that is *also* generated through participatory media. The history of the field has often been characterised by oscillating arguments about 'active' rather 'passive' audiences – which is a tension that is not at all resolved, but only further complicated by the mediatisation and digitisation of everything 'with simultaneously convergent and divergent, and centrifugal and centripetal consequences, on an increasingly global scale' (Livingstone, 2015: 1).

USES AND GRATIFICATIONS

Despite years of concentration on the negative effects of the mass media as described in Chapter 2, it was the 'uses and gratifications' tradition from the US that first presented the idea of audiences as active, posing the question, 'what do people do with the media?' The earliest 'uses and gratifications' traditions were concerned, from a psychological perspective, with how media were used to satisfy certain personal *needs* – it is important to note that 'use' here is derived from ideas about *individual* human needs – and research argued that 'people bend the media to their needs more readily than the media overpower them' (Katz, Gurevitch, and Haas, 1973: 268).

Research began to understand media consumption as directed by the diverse needs and motivations of audiences – therefore it aimed to open up the other side of the coin of effects research. For instance, 'uses and gratifications' studies suggested that soap operas help to reassure oneself of one's own role in life (Herzog, 1941), or newspapers

MEAN 61

satisfy a need for information which assists with the trials of daily life (Berelson, 1949), or that classical music on the radio helps people's endeavours in upwards mobility (Suchman, 1942). Denis McQuail's (1987) classic exploration of the uses and gratifications model has seen something of a revival in the contemporary landscape and it provides us with a typology which spans four realms of individual use based on needs that are fulfilled by the mass media: Information, Personal Identity, Integration and Social Interaction and Entertainment.

McQuail's original typology is not so different for digital culture where spaces for social interaction might not (even if they ever were) seen as substitutes for, but are rather integral to, social connection and communication. That original list of 'gratifications' drawn up in relation to mass media are remarkably similar to those found in research on internet users: interpersonal reasons, passing time, information-seeking and entertainment (Papacharissi and Rubin, 2000). What perhaps *is* most defining of the current conjuncture is the complexity with which we can mix some of these needs together quite easily in a converged media landscape as our searches for information or connection then lead us into interactive communication, debate or sociability. Some of what we achieve online we might now call 'mass self-communication' through which a tweet or post might reach a global audience online and is therefore 'mass communication' but it is also 'self' communication in that 'it is self-direction in the elaboration and sending of the message, self-directed in the reception of the message and self-defined in terms of the formation of the communication space' (Castells, 2007: 248 cited in McQuail and Deuze, 2020).

Audience researchers, perhaps without labelling themselves as uses and gratifications researchers, have developed new descriptions for these the ways in which we can move around or 'navigate' (Wood, 2007b) media platforms or inhabit transmedia worlds where multiple forms of engagement involve us 'roaming' across alternative spaces (Hill, 2019). Elizabeth Evans' (2020) research with audiences, draws out new behaviours associated with transmedia culture that involves ranging across texts and paratexts, and varying levels of commitment and intensity in modes of co-creation. Perhaps the way in which our needs are organised might not be directly related to discrete media as they once were, but even without framing the more recent entanglements of mass and interpersonal media, I would argue that interpersonal and mass-mediated communication was always entwined, embedded within social interactive fabrics, just as we can see in the example from *Gogglebox* above. This is reminiscent of my research *Talking with Television* in 2009 where my audience research participants regularly talked back to morning television talk shows. As Roger Silverstone reminded us when asking 'what's new about new media?' back in 1999, '*And any entry into electronic space has always presupposed and required physical space as both its beginning and its end point…* It is a simple law of any attempt to communicate' (1999: 10).

What I want to draw out however for the Cultural Studies researcher is not so much a psychological account of individual use and need – but a more contextually specific account of the dynamic nature of audience needs as they are socially derived. Needs surely change with social and cultural change. There has been some recognition that, 'affordances of media technology can shape users' needs, giving rise to new and distinct gratifications' (Sunder and Limperos, 2013: 521). Sunder and Limperos (2013) draw our attention to the multiple modalities afforded across an increased diversity of platforms. Uses and gratifications research now develops, largely via survey research, to consider the way in which new forms of sociability, sharing, information-seeking, etc. are generative across social media. For instance, how co-viewing and sharing on YouTube helps people feel connected (Haridakis and Hansen, 2009) or the ways sociability generates forms of social capital on Facebook (Papacharissi and Mendelson, 2011).

For Cultural Studies, we might also ask how these needs are also derived through the socio-political demands of the conjunctural context which includes, but is not entirely determined by, technological change. Some examples might be for instance: desires for self-performance and places to practice that; or increased needs for self-surveillance and the surveillance of others? Therefore it is not just a story of evolutionary change that heralds 'interactivity' as technological advancement, but it is in dialogue with the changing political contexts through which needs can be derived and manipulated, including the very terms for interactivity. So for instance, an increased desire for the observation of others, is also part of the way advanced capitalist societies have ideologically and politically encouraged a

MEAN 63

surveillant framework for living (see Chapter 1 Andrejevik, 2009). Even if we recognise that surveillance needs are enhanced, it is also worth noting that they were also identified as part of traditional and legacy media back in 1972 (McQuail, Blumler, and Brown, 1972). For the Cultural Studies audience researcher needs are interesting when they are recognised as produced through, and contingent upon, changing social and political contexts, and technological change is one part of a hermeneutic and dialectical process.

THE 'ACTIVE AUDIENCE' TRADITION OF CULTURAL STUDIES

The 'active audience' tradition is largely credited as emerging from a Gramscian-influenced critical position begun at the Centre for Contemporary Cultural Studies (CCCS) in Birmingham, UK, in the 1980s.[1] It was concerned with challenging models from political economy which it felt offered a reductionist account of the relationship between the mode of production and culture, taken from the work of Marx. Writing from the context of Thatcher's Britain, British Cultural Studies was influenced by the socio-economic and cultural shifts instilled via Thatcher's version of individualism which laid the groundwork for structural economic change (Jin, 2011).

There is not space here to recount fully all of the origins and institutional relationships that informed the interdisciplinary Cultural Studies audience traditions which were influenced by parallel literary as well as sociological lines of inquiry. However, the important distinction is that it took its theoretical starting point from concerns over the ideologies of the mass media from a perspective informed by Antonio Gramsci's ideas about hegemony. This position tried to understand the process by which the ideas of the ruling classes become the dominant and taken-for-granted ideas of any political epoch through the realm of culture. It pressed against what it saw as reductionist ideas from political economy which presumed the economy to have an entirely determining effect. The Cultural Studies tradition therefore was also *precisely* concerned with media content, ideologies and what audiences were making of them, putting *meaning-making* at the centre of its attempt to understand contemporary socio-cultural formations and focussing on various aspects of *interpretation* rather than *use*.

64 MEAN

Here political power is exercised also through cultural power and it becomes the responsibility of audience researcher to be concerned with how audiences *interpret* the meaning systems generated by the social and political contexts around them. This type of approach also laid the ground for acknowledging alternative modes of cultural expression that might even be able to resist dominant messages and ideas.

Central to this was Stuart Hall's (1980) 'encoding and decoding' model which also owed a great deal to the legacy of European work on semiotics in the cultural analysis of meaning. There exists more than one version of Hall's encoding/decoding essay (see Scannell, 2020), but the basic premise is that messages are doubly coded. At one end in the production of media content – which the media analyst may which wish to discern themselves using an analysis of its sign system – its broader cultural repertoire of meaning; and at the other end those messages are then decoded in the very 'social' contexts of reception through which is filtered through local contexts and experiences. This undermined older linear models of direct effects and acknowledged the idea that media messages are not necessarily consumed as they are intended. Audiences interpret and deconstruct those messages from within their very specific social locations – the broader contexts of their lives from which they also draw meaning opens up space for the audience to embody some form of resistive potential. Both of these processes, 'encoding and decoding', are central to communication, but we cannot at all assume that they are symmetrical. This model was at the centre of the 'circuit of culture' (Du Gay, 2013) which demonstrated how a cultural artefact went through a number of cultural processes (production, consumption, regulation, identity, representation), which worked together like a circuit in order to articulate a unity of meaning in any given culture, and to which we will return in Chapter 6.

The main difference here from the 'uses and gratifications' model is the language Cultural Studies used to analyse the audience: taste, value systems, and ideology are inherently *social* phenomenon that belong to an understanding of social structure, not individual in the sense that are prioritised by understanding personal individual psychological needs. Recent accounts of the uses and gratifications model

MEAN 65

acknowledge its problematic association with behaviourist models of media (see McQuail and Deuze, 2020).

David Morley (1980) first tested Hall's encoding/decoding theory in an investigation of the responses to the television programme *Nationwide* (a British early evening magazine current affairs television programme) with groups from different socio-demographic backgrounds. This work illustrated Hall's model with empirical data and found that different groups incorporated, negotiated or resisted, the preferred reading of the text, although there was still a rather complex picture through which those different reading positions emerged. This research has been one of the cornerstones of audience research in media and cultural studies and informs much of the work produced in the 1980s and 1990s which focussed on small-scale interviews and focus-groups identifying and theorising a number of 'interpretive communities' (Morley, 1992). This kind of work developed with an interest in the way in which media forms and their interpretations became resources for the construction of identity:

> Identity could be seen as dragging cultural studies into the 1990s by acting as a kind of guide to how people see themselves, not as class subjects, not as psychoanalytic subjects, but as active agents whose sense of self is projected onto and expressed in an expansive range of cultural practices, including texts, images and commodities.
>
> (McRobbie, 1992: 730 cited in Gray, 2006)

This opened the door for audience research into the relationship between media consumption and the formation of identities beyond the class structure, which had framed the earliest research.

The key distinction then between these two approaches to 'active audiences' (the approach to 'use' and the approach to 'meaning-making') is in Cultural Studies' main interest in the workings of power. Motivations in the research paradigms were different because uses and gratifications owed a great deal to the prominent perspective of functionalism from social science, which was popular in the 1940 and 1950s, particularly in the US and concentrated on how elements of a society worked together to maintain stability. Rather, Cultural Studies was concerned with how such a status quo was formed and maintained through culture and wanted to find the spaces for *challenging* the

66 MEAN

social structures and norms of society. For instance, when audience research interrogated the threat of cultural imperialism – the dominance of the Western media market over the rest of the world – audience research actually found 'resistance' to dominant ideologies from audiences on the ground (Liebes and Katz, 1990; Miller, 1993). Cultural Studies of the 1980s and 1990s was often criticised by political economy theorists for a position which ignored the economy and larger structures of power whilst overly celebrating the critical capacities of audiences in the long-running battles of the active/passive audience debates. For a good discussion of those debates at the time and the mis-reading of Cultural Studies' attention to the economy see Grossberg (1995).

CRITICAL AUDIENCE STUDIES

The Cultural Studies tradition has birthed a good deal of audience studies aligned with this more critical tradition. In particular, feminist research has played a dominant role in the production of Cultural Studies' audience research and in the creation of the field of media studies (Hermes, 2014). This research often turned to the terrain of the popular (as opposed to the news of the encoding/decoding model) where women's tastes and desires were considered trivial and dangerous for the ways in which they contributed to 'trapping' women within patriarchal consumer culture. The growth of what has often been termed the 'active audience' paradigm was sustained by feminist researchers who also wanted to defend the audience groups which they studied, producing analyses of resistive strategies of viewing and uncovering the types of value and sources of comfort that women found in popular media from within their restricted patriarchal conditions of existence (e.g. Hobson, 1982; Ang, 1984; Seiter, Borchers, and Warth, 1989; Press, 1991, Hermes, 1995; Gray, 1992 and from anthropology Mankekar, 1999).

Sut Jhally and Justin Lewis' (1993) work on audiences of the primetime sit-com *The Cosby Show* demonstrated the intersections of race and class as viewers critiqued the shows lack of socio-economic reality. Jacqueline Bobo's (1996) important work in *Black Women as Cultural Readers* discussed a group of African-American women's responses to texts like the film *The Colour Purple* which she suggests involves a complex series of negotiations that generated a community of readers who reconstruct the text in order to empower their social group. Youna Kim (2005) helps to decentre some of the Anglo-American dominance of these studies in her discussion of Korean women's reflexive relationships to television where generation, and to a lesser extent class, determine sets of relationships to television which she identifies as part of 'journeys of hope'. Concerned as it was with particular interpretative communities and often with marginalised voices, much of this work was conducted with direct concern for the questions of gender, race, class and sexuality.

In the development of queer audience research, Alexander Doty (2003) suggested through textual research that queer audiences perform queer readings of mainstream texts which were addressed to a heteronormative audiences in what has been terms the 'radical subversion' strain of queer media studies. But this has not always been followed up by many of examples of empirical audience research (Davis and Needham, 2009). However more recently in Alfred Martin's (2021) *The Generic Closet*, as well as considering the industrial production of the black gay-cast sitcom, his audience research shows how Black gay audiences understood the address of these sitcoms as not 'for them' as the black-gay characters were often de-centred and made props for the other characters. In these ways the audience members produced oppositional readings of the laugh-track as they recognised the address to an 'imagined Black heterosexual audience' (2021: 177). In Dhoest and Simons' (2011) research which comprised of questionnaires and interviews with gay audiences, they found that particular media uses were significant, especially during the process of 'coming out' but that actual resistive readings against heteronormative texts were more muted, and cautioned against assuming that 'radical subversion' from queer theory could be applied easily across the queer population. There are spaces though where queer audience studies celebrated the role of resistant interpretations, which were more likely to be found in fan fiction or slash fiction, where new readings, characters and storylines are created deliberately against heteronormative framings of the original text (Dhaenens, Bauwel, and Bilteryst, 2008).

However, more recently feminist media research has not engaged with audiences in the quite the same way – and there was an observably notable decline in audience research in a journal like *Feminist Media Studies* in the last decade (Cavalcante, Press, and Sender, 2017). Andre Cavalcante, Andrea Press and Katherine Sender therefore discuss what has become of feminist reception studies in a 'post-audience' age and point to the blurring of key categories – gender, the public and the private, and production and consumption – as all destabilising for empirical research. However, we can of course still see examples of feminist audience research which operate with insights drawn from those older legacies, for instance Melissa Click's (2015) analysis of how women used the popular soft-porn text *Fifty Shades of Grey* as a way to navigate contemporary 'hook-up' culture is reminiscent of Radway's earlier work on the way romance novels offer levels of 'support' to women in traditional relationships. Rebecca Feasey (2016) extends Dorothy Hobson's (1982) work which drew attention to the context of mothers then at home considers the reception of more contemporary representations of motherhood on television to consider how they navigate a range of issues from role models, discipline and domestic skills – and draws its framework from the changing landscape of television's address to mothers while querying the problems of inclusion and exclusion of motherhood as a category. Adrienne Shaw's (2014) research on how marginalised queer groups play video games draws on the tradition of feminist audience reception research to consider how in an era of diffuse, dispersed and interactive media, questions of representation and of identification still matter to the politics of sexuality. That research shows how feelings of being 'included' or being able to 'identify' with representations and avatars was relative to the way in which texts are used and accompanied by a broader attachment to questions of diversity per se. As Cavalcante, Press and Sender (2017) also point out feminist audience legacies are important to the contemporary development of the field, and are still important to the way in which we might think of 'audiencing' in the digital age.

THE ONGOING PROBLEM OF THE ACTIVE AUDIENCE

Some of the work from Cultural Studies that was given the label 'active audiences' came under fire for using John Fiske's ideas about the polysemic nature of media texts, which implied that that texts might be freely open to multiple readings depending upon one's social

MEAN 69

location. Research which used this insight to assume that the audience is easily able to retrieve and assume resistive readings of texts was often critiqued as overly celebratory of popular culture (Young, 1996) and sometimes for 'pointless populism' (Seaman, 1992). It is for attention to the particular combination of 'pleasure and resistance' that the active audience paradigm gained its name.

But it is important to remember that this was a particular moment in a research field, working to counter the ideas that audiences are necessarily 'cultural dopes' (Hall, 1981). Here 'action' refers to a reactionary position taken against media texts, but it is also often mooted from within or against the restrictive conditions of existence. Media texts are often used creatively as resources from the contexts that people find themselves in – whether that is Radway's mothers reading romance novels to create a nurturing space for their own care in patriarchal relationships, or *Star Trek* fans seeing opportunities afforded by re-writing mainstream sci-fi fiction so that it actually meets their sexual desires (Penley, 1997). The potential and possibilities opened up by fan activities has seen a huge body of literature interested in the way in which fan cultures have openly embraced the possibilities opened up by participatory culture (Bacon-Smith, 1992; Jenkins, 1992, 2006; Baym, 2002; Hills, 2002) The myriad ways in which texts are re-worked, intertextually interwoven through blogs, zines, GIF's, memes, Twitch sites etc. means that those once isolated texts are now multiplied and scattered across multiple sites and spaces, contributing to a range of more trans-mediated and multi-mediated audience practices. Paul Booth (2016) in his two editions of *Digital Fandom* gives us a detailed account of the ways in which fan practices are developing in step with new technological affordances into more dynamic modes of engagement from blogs to platforms like Tumblr which he argues has 'revolutionised fandom' (2016: 4). So prolific is fan activity that the phrase 'active audience' seems rather redundant given the multiple ways in which audiences and fans can engage and interact online as they embrace a 'participation paradigm' (Livingstone, 2013).

Yet the tendency I have described in previous chapters, to observe large scale shifts from the mass analogue audience to the more niche and fragmented digital audiences of the internet era have sometimes overlooked the continuities between these traditions of active audiences. As Livingstone and Das (2013) helpfully pointed out, the

70 MEAN

growth of interest in 'new media users' from areas outside of media studies (science and technology studies, human–computer interaction, library and information studies and so on) has meant that quite often any connection between the 'active audience' of television and the computer user would have been overlooked. Re-articulated questions of 'use' seem to operate without a memory of older questions of 'interpretation'.

Indeed, the rise of internet studies and early 'new media studies' in over-looking these traditions of audience research, seemed to undo some of the gains made in resisting ideas of 'audience passivity'. For some proponents of the 'new media studies' of the 1990s, the television audience became realigned with the passivity of the couch potato (popular in the 1950s), whilst the internet 'user' was framed as an active 'netizen' associated more closely with active citizenship and even revolutionary potential (Dewdney and Ride, 2006).

Action here seems only palpable when aligned with the more physical framework of *communicative* interactivity. Television is a one-way medium whilst the internet allows more participatory interaction – but of course all interactions are not necessarily even, and all interaction might also involve and enact uneven power dynamics. As we saw in Chapter 1 'interactivity' itself as some kind of panacea is not necessarily the route to more equal participation and is contingent upon the forms and modalities by which it is put to use in the service of overarching power relations.

ATTENDING TO *FORM*

As Martin Barker (2006) pointed out, audience research conducted on the ground, tends to overturn and challenge over-generalised certainties about grand shifts in audience behaviour, or settled accounts of engagements with texts and technologies. One of the key issues that we might observe here is that Cultural Studies was traditionally more aligned with questions of the interpretation of meaning which drew upon the legacies of semiotics and linguistics in its concern for the textual determination and interpretation of meaning, whilst as new media studies emerged it was concerned more with technology, 'use' and technological affordances. But of course the way we use media and the ways in which we interpret their messages as processes are not easily disentangled when we try to understand how we live *with* media. This was true even when we dealt with more discrete media objects and texts as part of older media systems: Novels are materially objects of comfort as they tell us stories of patriarchal romance, television as a technology and form offers us some ontological security as a way of anchoring ourselves in the world as dramas and talk shows reaffirm our ways of life, and this is still similar to the ways that communities of gamers might be reassured in their interactions and sense of belonging around 'Lets Play' on YouTube.

Power circulates through all of these 'engagements' where meaning systems and uses are entangled in and through sometimes compensatory practices for dominant social structures, but we need also to bear in mind the social contexts and the terrain of inequalities through which any meaning-making practices must operate. Recall earlier how we discussed the way in which in the uses and gratifications tradition imagines the way in which social change is closely tied in the production of individual needs. In 1973 Katz, Blumler, and Gurevitch (1973) asked, 'what needs if any are created by routine work on an assembly line, and which forms of media exposure will satisfy them?' (1973: 516). McQuail, Blumer, and Brown (1972) suggested that those who reported 'educational appeal' as a major gratification of media had left school at the minimum age. Questions of use are not neutrally floating around, and we are not 'free' to use the media in any way we wish – our needs and desires are mutually produced in relation to the socio-cultural and political conjuncture and the uneven social order within which we are situated. Much like some of the arguments by feminist works on popular culture, the media might offer compensatory practices, gratifying needs that are frustrated by other structures of social life (Fiske, 1992) but they also generate new sentiments and feelings, which harbour potential for agency and activity that is not always predictable to the audience researcher (see Chapter 4).

One of the reasons why these two realms – of meaning-making and media use – have in the past seemed so distinct, is related to the earlier dominance of semiotics over the field of media studies, as much as it was related to any technological change. The idea that in media texts, we can attempt to discern some stable meaning systems via a more structuralist account of semiotics through a linguistic interpretative

72 MEAN

frame meant that many audience reception studies assumed a similar text–reader relationship adopted from literary studies that was never always appropriate the way all media forms are lived and experienced in social contexts (Wood, 2009). This may indeed have contributed to the idea that these models seem outmoded for a more participatory and interactive environment which is characterised by a plethora of uses, engagements and interactions.

My attention to form joins John Corner's (2011) plea to elevate form from its more 'secondary' status and to give it a much more 'pivotal' place in media research. Attention to form tends to focus on medium-specificity and speaks to the structure of genre and style, as well as questions of sound and aesthetics as opposed to straight-forward 'content'. Form as the 'mode in which a thing…manifests itself' (2011: 50) is often registered mostly in relation to media objects, or texts or medium, but I want to make clear here its importance for audience analysis. In Corner's (2011) discussion he describes three dynamics of form, organisation, articulation and apprehension

> *Organisation* raises questions about the production of form but also about its objectified deployment as a necessary constituent of discursive and aesthetic artefacts. *Articulation* raises questions about form as performance, giving to the term a marked sense of process and practice. *Apprehension* gives emphasis to engagement with form by viewers and readers, *the dynamic by which formal factors become active in the in the production of knowledge and emotion, in the complex subjective interactions of our media encounters* which are part of our larger, continuous immersion in mediation.'
>
> (2011: 50 my emphasis)

The formal structures of any mediated product become central to the ways in which they are apprehended, understood and generative of subjectivities on the ground. My own research on the reception of television talk shows in the home *Talking With Television* (2009) argued that broadcasting was not always easy to analyse with any stable meaning (content) structure, especially for talk-based television. We need also to consider the *form* of this kind of television and the way in which it adopted communicative styles, what Scannell (2000) in his attention to broadcasting form called 'anyone-as-someone' structures.

These approximate interaction across the broadcast setting and assume 'para-social relations' even if they are not interactive in the sense that the audience can determine the direction of the media output. My research demonstrated 'para-social' arrangements – that were often researched more as part of the uses and gratifications paradigm – as established between the home and the television studio. The women in the study felt conversationally included into the show and they answered questions from the studio, joined in conversational turns, shouted back at participants and presenters, 'putting them straight', and it required an approach to pragmatics as much as to semiotics to consider just how meaning is established in what I described as the 'mediated conversational floor' (Wood, 2007). My fieldwork was carried out in the late 1990s some time before the inception of Channel 4's Gogglebox (2013–) the TV show which captures the dramatic potential of audiences reacting to their television set with which we opened this chapter.

The point here is that it is the *form* of the talk shows that also generates the meanings for audiences. What Fiske described as 'textuality' – the space through which meaning is generated as texts come alive through their interaction with audiences – has potential to be opened up through close attention to the *form* that the particular media or medium takes. In this case this allowed me a way into understanding textual negotiations with audiences, using methods which differed from the more standard approach to interviews or focus groups that asked audiences how they 'interpreted' the text. Capturing live engagements as mediated conversation through a methodology I called the 'text-in-action' allowed me to see immediacy, as central to television's form, and meaning system.

It is this *form* which allows my audiences into the ideological world of meaning in talk shows, one which privileged ideologies of self-disclosure and narratives of self-reflexivity as vitally part of the neoliberal architecture which proscribes feminised individual therapeutic solutions to the wider structural problems of the 1990s (White, 1994). Here we can see that subjectivity and textuality are complexly imbricated (Wood, 2005) which seems to reinforce the models of theorising that were holding sway at the time, for instance Anthony Giddens' (1991) theorisation that contemporary society involves the

74 MEAN

dis-embedding and the re-embedding of social relationships. But this audience work on the ground also challenged his conclusion that dis-embedding necessarily 'propels social life away from the hold of pre-established precepts or practices' (1991: 20). My work shows how the form of this television genre encourages women to rehearse their gendered selves as wives, mothers, and carers: in short re-embedding can mean the mediation of relatively fixed notions of womanhood. There is not necessarily an inevitable link between self-reflexivity and individualisation, and others have argued that processes of individual-isation have tended to re-make, rather than undo, classed and gendered distinctions (Adkins, 2003; Skeggs, 2004).

Following John Corner therefore matters of form in media analysis suggests 'a process whereby meanings are generated by intersecting dynamics' (2011: 51). It made no sense in my research to think about 'use' and 'interpretation' as entirely separate questions. The conver-sational imperative to feel part of a communicative group with shared experiences serves personal social functions that are also inextricably tied to political ones. I want the reader to hold onto this account of form for Chapter 6 and its ongoing usefulness to help us to account for our engagements with interfaces and platforms in the digital envir-onment because it 'also allows a proper consideration of technology both as a key factor in the availability and application of the formal options with which producers work, and a factor in defining the nature of mediation as an experience for readers and viewers [and we might add users], through various devices of domestic and personal delivery' (Corner 2011: 51/52).

THE ETHNOGRAPHIC SENSIBILITY

While traditional Cultural Studies audience research has indeed mapped a series of 'interpretive' communities in relation to par-ticular texts, the influence of a concern with everyday life and with 'lived experiences' saw an important turn to ethnography. In *Family Television* David Morley (1986) proposed the need to understand the social contexts through which people received the media, echoing a broader interest in ethnographic traditions from anthropology into the study of 'alien' cultures, sociologists and media researchers took to more embedded methods for understanding the appropriation of

MEAN 75

media objects and forms. Morley's (1986) study describes the way in which family power dynamics impact upon the *use* of the television set and choices of programming. Similarly James Lull's (1990) research on the *social* uses of television, based on ethnographic research, produced a typology of both the structural and relational uses of television that is not entirely dissimilar to some of the premises of audience motivations that we saw in the uses and gratifications from Denis McQuail. The early feminist media research such as Dorothy Hobson's (1980) work on young British mothers' use of the media in the home, addressed the gender politics of mothering and domestic responsibility within which media combats loneliness and structures the repetitive tasks of housework. Joke Hermes (1995) study with Dutch women magazine readers showed that their interpretative repertoires were also embedded within the unremarkable rituals of the everyday. Ann Gray's (1992) study on British women's use of video cassette recorder demonstrated the way in which the technology became part of the gendered power relations of labour in the home. These studies also had questions of 'use' at their heart, but these were firmly structured around local dynamics and power-relations through small scale ethnographic studies.

Whilst questions of 'use' have more often been to tied interactions with technology and the interpretations of cultural meaning associated with the reception of texts, ethnographic research in this tradition also often demonstrated how these concerns were not easily separable in lived experience, especially when relying on anthropological methods of 'thick description' (Geertz, 1973). For instance, Marie Gillespie's (1995) study of schoolchildren living in Southall in London UK, discusses the various ways in which television as text and technology is used in the negotiation of diasporic experience and in the power struggles between generations. Thomas Tufte's (2000) research on women living in the favelas of Brazil shows how the technology itself marked the significatory and permeable boundary between home and street, whilst the narratives of the popular telenovelas were appropriated and related to personal struggles and hopes for change. Purnima Mankekar's (1999) ethnography on the role of television in Indian women's lives, demonstrates the ways in which text and socio-political context are intricately interwoven. She describes how images from traditional series like *Mhabharat* resonate so emotionally with women viewers that they were able to 'confront and theorize their own vulnerabilities as women' (1999: 256) from within the context of increasing violence of the Indian state. The richness of these findings, where structural political formations, media forms and their social contexts come to bear upon individual lives, can only really be generated by a method which relies on intensive and localised periods of ethnographic data collection.

Media ethnographies have therefore developed with various influences from anthropology and sociology, drawing in such related theoretical positions. Shaun Moores (1993) for instance called for a greater sensitivity to the work of Pierre Bourdieu and the way in which habitus and questions of the 'feel' for the game can help us to explore how media *practices* embed themselves within everyday life. (The work of Pierre Bourdieu and the application of theories of taste its relation to social structure has played a considerable role in the formation of audience and fan research, which we will return to in Chapter 4.)

When dealing with increasingly globalised and transnational populations for instance, such sensitivities to locality and place, of the kind derived from anthropology, become even more central. Jansson (2013) argues for a turn to Bourdieu's reflexive sociology to help explain cosmopolitan sensitivities on the ground when dealing with media experiences and transnational flows. Work on 'polymedia' as described by Mirca Madianou (2014) has been helpful to our understanding of the role media technologies play as they mutually produce the contexts of transnational lives – for example in the lives of mothers working as nannies, skyping and contacting their own children as they parent across the screen. Research on the very complex patterns of contemporary migration and the experiences of being 'in-between' worlds, waiting and senses of belonging are discussed through complex attachments to both media forms and media technologies as the axis through which politics, rights as well as sensibilities of 'home' and movement is filtered (Twigt, 2018a, b). Cunningham and Sinclair's (2000) work on *Floating Lives* researched the role of the media in a range of migrant populations in Australia in order to inform the scope and production of media for those populations.

Working with an ethnographic sensibility therefore tends to eschew binaries between techno-celebratory and techno-pessimistic accounts

MEAN   77

of our lives with media in these transnational contexts. For instance, Gillespie, Osseiran, and Cheesman's (2018) analysis of Syrian and Iraqi refugees' use of smartphones elucidates the more fine-grained interplay between elements of control generated by surveillant architectures where bodies can be monitored and tracked to the more restorative affordances used as people cope and navigate complex everyday lives.

The centrality of context has led some to a call for a complete move away from an emphasis upon particular media and particular texts into what has been called 'non-media centric' media studies which begins with experience and contextualisation, rather than with particular media or technologies (see Krajina, Moores, and Morley, 2014; Moores, 2018). This is a call which works past more static models of representation that were available to the early Cultural Studies researcher, originally drawn from an emphasis upon semiotic meaning-systems. I am here glossing a series of key debates in the development of ethnographies of media reception and their relationship to anthropology, but the point is that the level of media complexity has also evolved to meet the audience researcher, and so too has the dissolution of any easy separation between inquiries into questions of 'use' and 'interpretation'. What emerges is that in attending to the hyper-complexity which now drives the field, as we discussed in Chapter 1, we must also be attuned to the ways in which meaning-systems are generated and created in engagements with media, which combine the discursive (symbolic), the communicative (sociable and interactive), the material (including the technological and contextual) and the experiential (ways of being in the world). We will think more closely about how to put these things together in our research into audiences in the final chapter of the book.

CONCLUSION

We opened this chapter with the question: *How should the researcher approach the overlapping processes of meaning-making?* What I have tried to do here is give the reader an account of the legacies of audience research that first gave us the notion of an 'active audience' and suggest their ongoing relevance for the contemporary conjuncture. I then drew on my own research and argued for a much closer attention to 'form' as a tool in our audience analysis, because form can begin to tell us something more of the precise relationship between media specificity and its apprehension in reception which is useful for future research on platforms and architectures. My research in the 2000s was a challenge to ideas about interactivity as the panacea of the internet age, since it complicated any easy assumption about a paradigmatic technological shift to interactivity, whilst also demonstrating how uses and interpretations are interwoven in the fabric of our experiences with media. In the conclusion to the book *Talking With Television* (2009) I argued for consideration of the term 'mechanics' – a system of mutually adapted parts – as a more fluid metaphor with which to capture the nature of audience engagements with specific media, which we will return to in Chapter 6. This, we might suggest allows for a broad way to capture the scope of 'audienceing' in the current moment as it is bound up in representational and non-representational systems, drawing from pragmatics as much as semiotics, understanding performances as much as interpretations, generating pictures of reactions, interactions, engagements, interventions, participations, for what they tell us about the social world around us.

For the Cultural Studies audience researcher, the commitment to 'audiencing' must always be attuned to socio-political formation and must remember to be radically contextual – to combine the discursive (symbolic) and the communicative (sociable and interactive) with the material (including the technological and contextual) and experiential (the ways of being in the world) in these complex overlapping dynamics where meaning is made. In collecting together some fruitful ways to grasp audience complexity – there is another useful verb which helps us to 'see' conjunctural relations – that is the usefulness of 'feeling' and 'affective registers' to which we will turn in the next chapter.

NOTES

1 The cultural studies tradition from Birmingham was also in conversation with mass communications traditions, particular as being practiced at the Leicester Centre for Mass Communications Research. In fact that relationship was more generative and sometimes more collaborative than is often acknowledged (Wood, 2016).

REFERENCES

Adkins, L. (2003) 'Reflexivity: Freedom or Habit of Gender?', *Theory, Culture & Society*, 20(6), 21–42.

Andreyevic, M. (2009) *ISpy: Surveillance and Power in the Interactive Era*. Kansas, University of Kansas Press.

Ang, I. (1984) *Watching Dallas: Soap Opera and the Melodramatic Imagination*. London: Methuen.

Bacon-Smith, C. (1992) *Enterprising Women: Television Fandom and the Creation of Popular Myth*. Pennysylvania, PA: University of Pennsylvania Press.

Barker, M. (2006) 'I have seen the future and it is not here yet... Or, on being ambitious for audience research', *Communication Review* 9 (2): 123–141.

Baym, N.K. (2002) *Tune In log On: Soap Fandom and Online Community*. Thousand Oaks, CA: Sage.

Berelson, B. (1949) 'What "missing the newspaper" means', in Lazarsfeld, P.F. and Stanton, F.N. (eds.) *Communications Research 1948-9*. New York: Duell Sloan and Pearce, pp. 111–129.

Booth, P. (2016) *Digital Fandom 2.0*. New York: Peter Lang.

Castells, M. (2007) 'Communication, power and counter-power in the network society', *International Journal of Communication* 1: 238–266.

Cavalcante, A., Press, A. and Sender, K (2017) 'Feminist reception studies in a post-audience age: Returning to audiences and everyday life', *Feminist Media Studies*, 17(1): 1–13. doi: 10.1080/14680777.2017.1261822.

Click, M. A. (2015) 'Fifty Shades of postfeminism: Contextualizing readers' reflections on the erotic romance series', in E. Levine (Ed.) *Cupcakes, Pinterest, Ladyporn: Feminized Popular Culture in the Early 21st Century*. Urbana: University of Illinois Press, pp. 15–31.

Corner, J. (2011) *'Form' in Theorising Media: Power, Form and Subjectivity*. Manchester: Manchester University Press.

Cunningham, S. and Sinclair, J. (2000) *Floating Lives: Media and Asian Diasporas*. Brisbane: University of Queensland Press.

Du Gay, P. et al. (2013) *Doing Cultural Studies: The Story of the Sony Walkman* (second edition). London and New York: Sage.

Davis, G. and Needham, G. (2009) 'Introduction: The pleasure of the tube', in Davis, G. and Needham, G. (eds.) *Queer TV: Theories, Histories, Politics* Abingdon: Routledge, pp. 1–11.

Deuze, M. and McQuail, D. (2020) *McQuail's Media and Mass Communication Theory*. London: Sage.

Dewdney, A. and Ride, P. (2006) *The New Media Handbook*. London: Routledge.

Dhaenens, F., Bauwel, S.V., and Bilteryst, D. (2008) 'Slashing the fiction of queer theory: Slash fiction, queer reading and transgressing the boundaries of screen studies, representations and audiences', *Journal of Communication Inquiry* 32 (4): 335–347.

Dhoest, A. and Simons, N. (2011) 'Questioning queer audiences: exploring diversity in lesbian and gay men's media uses and readings', in Ross, K. (ed.) *The Handbook of Gender, Sex and Media*. Sussex: Wiley-Blackwell, pp. 260–276.

80 MEAN

Doty, A. (2003) *Making Things Perfectly Queer: Interpreting Mass Culture*. Minneapolis, MN: University of Minnesota Press.

Evans, E. (2020) *Understanding Engagement in Transmedia Culture*. London: Routledge.

Feasey, R. (2016) *Mothers on Mothers: Maternal Readings of Popular Television*. Bristol, Peter Lang.

Fiske, J. (1992) 'The Cultural Economy of Fandom', in Lisa A. Lewis (ed.) *The Adoring Audience: Fan Culture and Popular Media*, London: Routledge. p. 256.

Geertz, C. (1973) *The Interpretation of Cultures* Basic Books. New York.

Giddens, A. (1991) *Modernity and Self Identity: Self and Society in the Modern Age*. London, Polity.

Gillespie, M. (1995) *Television, Ethnicity and Cultural Change*. London: Routledge.

Gillespie, M., Osseiran, S., and Cheesman, M. (2018) 'Syrian refugees and the digital passage to Europe: Smartphone infrastructures and affordances', *Social Media + Society* 4 (1): 1–12.

Gray, A. (1992) *Video Playtime: The Gendering of a Leisure Technology*. London: Routledge.

Grossberg, L. (1995) 'Cultural studies vs. political economy: Is anybody else bored with this debate?', Critical Studies in Mass Communication 12 (1): 72–81.

Hall, S. (1980) 'Encoding/Decoding', in Hall, S., et al. (eds.) *Culture, Media, Language: Working Papers in Cultural Studies*. London: Hutchinson, pp. 128–138.

Hall, S. (1981) "Notes on deconstructing 'the popular', in Samuel, R. (ed.) *People's History and Socialist Theory*. London: Routledge and Kegan Paul, pp. 227–240.

Haridakis, P. and Hanson, G. (2009). 'Social interaction and co-viewing with YouTube: Blending mass communication reception and social connection', *Journal of Broadcasting & Electronic Media* 53: 317–335. http://dx.doi.org/10.1080/08838150902908270

Hermes, J. (1995) *Reading Women's Magazines: An Analysis of Everyday Media Use*. Cambridge: Polity Press.

Hermes, J. (2014) 'Rediscovering twentieth century feminist audience research', in Carter, C., McLaughlin, L., and Steiner, L. (eds.) *The Routledge Companion to Media and Gender*. New York: Routledge, pp. 61–70.

Herzog, H. (1941) 'Motivations and gratifications of daily serial listeners', in Schramm, W. and Roberts, D. (eds.) *The Process and Effects of Mass Communication* (Revised 1971). Champaign, IL: University of Illinois Press, pp. 50–55.

Hill, A. (2019) *Media Experiences: Engaging with Drama and Reality Television*. London: Routledge.

Hills, M. (2002) *Fan Cultures*. New York: Routledge.

Hobson, D. (1980) 'Housewives and the mass media', in Hall, S., et al. (eds.) *Culture, Media, Language*. London: Hutchinson, pp. 104–114.

Hobson, D. (1982) *Crossroads: The Drama of a Soap Opera*. London: Methuen.

Jansson, A. (2013) 'A second birth? Cosmopolitan media ethnography and Bourdieu's reflexive sociology', *International Journal of Cultural Studies* 16 (2): 135–150.

Jenkins, H. (1992) *Textual Poachers: Television Fans and Participatory Culture*. New York: Routledge.

Jenkins, H. (2006) *Convergence Culture: Where Old and New Media Collide*. New York: New York University Press.

Jhally, S. and Lewis, J. (1993) *Enlightened Racism: The Cosby Show, Audiences and The Myth of the American Dream*. Boulder, CO: Westview Press.

Jin, H. (2011) 'British cultural studies, active audiences and the status of cultural theory: An interview with David Morley', *Theory, Culture & Society*, 28(4): 124–144.

Katz, E., Blumler, J. G., & Gurevitch, M. (1973). Uses and Gratifications Research. The Public Opinion Quarterly, 37(4), 509–523. http://www.jstor.org/stable/2747854

Katz, E., Gurevitch, M., & Haas, H. (1973). On the use of the mass media for important things. *American Sociological Review*, 38(1), 31-65.

Kim, Y. (2005) *Women, Television and Everyday Life in Korea: Journeys of Hope*. Routledge Advances in Korean Studies. London and New York: Routledge.

Krajina, Z., Moores, S., and Morley, D. (2014) 'Non-media-centric media studies: A cross-generational conversation', *European Journal of Cultural Studies* 17 (6): 682–700. https://doi.org/10.1177/1367549414526733

Liebes, T. and Katz, E. (1990) *The Export of Meaning*. Oxford: Oxford University Press

Livingstone, S. (2013) 'The participation paradigm in audience research', *The Communication Review* 16: 21–30.

Livingstone, S. (2015) 'Active audiences?: The debate progresses but it is far from resolved', *Communication Theory* 25 (4): 1–7.

Lull, J. (1990) *Inside Family Viewing*. London: Routledge.

Madioanou, M. (2014) 'Polymedia communication and mediatized migration: An ethnographic approach', in Lundby, K. (ed.) *Mediatization of Communication* (pp. 323–348). Berlin: De Gruyter.

Mankekar, P. (1999) *Screening Culture: Viewing Politics: An Ethnography of Television, Womanhood and Nation in Postcolonial India*. Durham, NC: Duke University Press.

Martin, A., Jr. (2021) *The Generic Closet: Black Gayness and the Black-Cast Sitcom*. Bloomington, IN: Indiana University Press.

McQuail, D. (1987) *Mass Communication Theory: An introduction*. London: Sage.

McQuail, D., Blumler, J.G., and Brown, J.R. (1972) 'The television audience: A revised perspective', in McQuail, D. (ed.) *Sociology of Mass Communications*. Harmondsworth: Penguin, pp. 135–165.

McRobbie, A. (1992) 'Post-marxism and cultural studies: A post-script', in Grossberg, L., Nelson, C., and Treichler, P. (eds.) *Cultural Studies*. New York: Routledge, pp. 719–730.

Miller, D. (1993) 'The young and the restless in Trinidad: A case study of the local and the global in media consumption', in Silverstone, R. and Hirsch, E. (eds.) *Consuming Technologies*. London: Routledge, pp. 163–182.

Moores, S. (1993) *Interpreting Audiences: The Ethnography of Media Consumption* London: Sage.

Moores, S. (2018) *Digital Orientations: Non-Media-Centric Media Studies and Non-Representational Theories of Practice*. Bern: Peter Lang.

Morley, D. (1980) *The Nationwide Audience*. London: BFI.

Morley, D. (1986) *Family Television: Cultural Power and Domestic Consumption*. London: Comedia.

Morley, D. (1992) *Television, Audiences and Cultural Studies*. London: Routledge.

Papacharissi, Z. and Mendelson, A. (2011) 'Toward a new(er) sociability: Uses, gratifications and social capital on Facebook', in Papathanassopoulis, S. (ed.) *Media Perspectives for the 21st Century*. New York: Routledge, pp. 212–230.

Papacharissi, Z. and Rubin, A. (2000) 'Predictors of internet research', *Journal of Broadcasting and Electronic Media* 44: 175–196.

Penley, C. (1997) *Nasa Trek Popular Science and Sex in America*. London and New York: Verso Books.

Press, A.L. (1991) *Women Watching Television Gender, Class, and Generation in the American Television Experience*. Pennsylvania, PA: University of Pennsylvania Press.

Radway, J. (1984) *Reading the Romance: Women, Patriarchy and Popular Literature*. Chapel Hill, NC: North Carolina University Press.

Seaman, W.R. (1992) 'Active audience theory: Pointless populism', *Media, Culture and Society* 14: 301–311.

Scannell, P. (2000) 'For-anyone-as-someone structures', *Media, Culture & Society* 22 (1): 5–24.

Scannell, P. (2020) *Media and Communication* (second edition). London and New York: Sage.

Seiter, E., Borchers, H., and Warth, E. (1989) 'Don't treat us like we are so stupid and naive: Towards an ethnography of soap opera viewers', in Seiter, E., et al. (eds.) *Remote Control: Television, Audiences and Cultural Power*. London: Routledge, pp. 223–247.

Shaw, A. (2015) *Gaming at the Edge: Sexuality and Gender at the Margins of Gamer Culture*. Minneapolis, MN: University of Minnesota Press.

Skeggs, B. (2004) *Class, Self, Culture*. London: Routledge.

Silverstone, R. (1999) 'What's new about new media', *New Media and Society* 1: 10–11.

Suchman, E. (1942) 'An invitation to music', in Lazarsfeld, P.F. and Stanton F.N. (eds.) *Radio Research, 1941*. New York: Deuell, Sloan and Pearce 140–188.

Sunder, S. and Limperos, A. (2013) 'Uses and grats 2.0: New gratifications for new media', *Journal of Broadcast and Electronic Media* 57 (4): 504–525.

Thomas, T. (2000) *Living With the Rubbish Queen: Telenovelas and Modernity in Brazil*. Luton: University of Luton Press.

Twigt, M. (2018a) *The Mediation of Prolonged Displacement in the Iraqi Refugee Household in Jordan*. University of Leicester PhD thesis.

Twigt, M. (2018b) 'The mediation of hope: Digital technologies and affective affordances within Iraqi refugee households in Jordan', *Social Media Society* 4 (1): 205630511876442.

White, R.A. (1994) 'Audience interpretation of media: Emerging perspectives', *Communication Research Trends* 14 (3): 3–36.

Wood, H. (2005) 'Texting the subject: Women, television and modern self-reflexivity', Communication Review 8(2): 115–135.

Wood, H. (2007a) 'The mediated conversational floor: An interactive approach to audience reception analysis', *Media, Culture & Society* 29 (1): 75–103.

Wood, H. (2007b) 'Television is happening: Method"dological considerations for capturing digital television reception', *European Journal of Cultural Studies* 10 (4): 485–506.

Wood, H. (2009) *Talking With Television: Women, Talking Shows and Modern Self-Reflexivity*. Urbana, IL: University Press.

Wood, H. (2016) '50 years of Media and Communication Research at Leicester, UK', IAMCR international conference Leicester UK.

Young, L. (1996) 'Jacqueline Bobo, Black Women as cultural readers; Marie Gillespie, television, ethnicity and cultural change', *Screen* 37 (4): 400–408. https://doi.org/10.1093/screen/37.4.400

Zuboff, S. (2019) *The Age of Surveillance Capitalism: The Fight for a Human Future at the New Frontier of Power*. New York: PublicAffairs.

4

FEEL

SCENARIO: KPOP FANDOM

In September 2021, the hashtag #KpopTwitter amassed a whopping 7.8 billion tweets – a number equivalent to the world's total population.[1] As a cultural phenomenon Hallyu, the Korean Wave of popular music, has proved a huge global success, spawning an army of globally connected fans and a new dawn of 'K-Pop studies' (Yoon et al., 2017). K-Pop fans such as the 'BTS Army' take to social media, Instagram, X/Twitter, Facebook and TikTok to demonstrate their love for their idols, their styling, as well as their music. At the centre of the process they practice their own creativity, generating content to demonstrate their love but also to help drive up the popularity of their favourite group and stars. Known for its pushing at gender boundaries K-pop stardom has spawned an army of fans, many from LGBTQ+ communities, taking what was once a fairly marginal set of 'alternative' attachments to a national music style, into the global mainstream.

I am drawing on this example here because it is emblematic of two things that are important for this chapter. First, the power of feelings of love and connection towards and around media products, and here K-Pop idols, to generate forms of connection and community

DOI: 10.4324/9781003414575-5

in practices of identity-building (see Chapter 3). Second, because it tells us of the power of social media platforms to amplify and extend those affective attachments into places and formations that could not necessarily be predicted. One of the most intriguing things about K-Pop fandom is the way in which it has developed into K-Pop activism. In 2020, K-Pop fans took to TikTok to encourage fans to reserve free tickets to a Donald Trump rally in Tulsa Oklahoma in order to leave many of the 19,000 seats empty in protest against the right wing politician.[2] K-Pop fans have subsequently worked on anti-racist campaigns, drowning out racist commentary on the #WhiteLivesMatter hashtag and responding to Asian hate campaigns during the Covid pandemic helping the hashtag #StopAsianHate reach 1million tweets in 2021. This example is revealing of numerous insights into developments in audience relations, and in particular their increasingly transnational and globalised character and the reach and potential of participatory culture, as discussed in Chapter 1. However, I want to draw on K-Pop fandom here primarily in order to think through the importance of feelings in relation to audience engagements and how their analysis can help to inform our understanding of the politics of social change.

QUESTION: WHAT CAN FEELINGS TELL US ABOUT MEDIA AUDIENCES AND CHANGING SOCIAL RELATIONS?

Audiences form personal attachments to particular kinds of media and medium just as the K-Pop fans above. Continued affection for the material vinyl of records in the era of streaming services and Spotify tells us something of the way in which those attachments can be deeply felt, lived and nurtured, and how they are central to the processes of identity and belonging into the digital age. Throughout the history of audience research, relationships with media have always been intricately connected to questions of emotion and feeling. Consider the ways in which the analyses of crowds discussed in Chapter 2 was concerned with the foreboding potential of the emotional fervour of people gathering together; or recall in Chapter 3 the way in which the 'uses and gratifications' researcher was often concerned with the

86 FEEL

media's role in ameliorating personal feelings like 'loneliness'. Popular and sometimes academic accounts of the overwhelming abundance of endless information and connectivity of social media leads to some to suggest that it is generating boredom, anxiety and despair – apps are basically making us sad in their very design (Lovink, 2019). However, Susannah Paasonen (2021) in *Dependant, Distracted, Bored* tells us to be cautious of such certainty and to pay closer attention to the ambiguities at the heart of affective formations in digital culture where, 'frustration and pleasure, dependence and a sense of possibility, distraction and attention, boredom, interest and excitement enmesh, oscillate, enable and depend on one another' (2021: 4).

The social sciences have developed considerable theoretical insights into the analysis of emotion and 'affect' (the felt bodily responses in society and culture) in what has been termed an 'affective turn' to our analysis (Clough and Halley, 2007). However, that turn is less singular than it appears and is in fact more a messy 'series of turns' (Hills, Paasonen and Petit, 2015). This work on affect has the potential to generate analytical accounts of the relationship between physiological responses to media, the way in which affects move between bodies, and their social and political implications. But it is important to note that attention to the 'feelings' of a culture and what they tell us about the social and political contexts of cultural formation, have a longer history in the field of Cultural Studies. Raymond Williams in *The Long Revolution* (1961) developed his earlier use of the phrase 'structure of feeling' to account for the ways in which popular sentiment emerges in response to more official and public discourses in order to complicate Antonio Gramsci's more settled account of the structuring of hegemony and ideology (Chapter 3). Gramsci's account of hegemony referred to the importance of culture to the working of ideology – away from the more economistic accounts of Marx, but for Raymond Williams, hegemony can never be complete or totalising. This is a useful starting point for how we understand feelings as they pertain to audiences, as nascent responses to media narratives and events, which are not necessarily fully-formed responses to 'official discourses', but have the potential to capture insights into the developing conjunctural moment.

In this chapter, I will set out some of the ways in which feelings have been central to different forms of audience analysis, beginning with questions of taste and fandom, as well as drawing upon feminist audience studies traditions that have placed the emotional realm at the centre of their analysis. I then move to consider the influence the attention to the 'affective turn' in social and cultural theory and its usefulness to my own research on reality television audiences and class (Skeggs and Wood, 2012). I will conclude this chapter with an account of some of the more recent applications of affect in the analysis of social media, including the notion of affective contagion and the generation of 'affective publics' (Papacharizzi, 2014), arguing that there are through-lines and overlaps between 'traditional' audience research and social media analysis. Whilst it is impossible to offer an exhaustive account of all related directions to the analytical power of feeling in audience research, using our compass of 'audiencing', I want to argue for an approach that draws our attention to what emotion tells us about everything else – in terms of the socio-political conjuncture that is central to Cultural Studies.

TASTE AND VALUE

Since I am mostly concerned with what feelings can tell us about social and cultural formations, I am going to start here with fundamental questions of taste, what we 'like' and don't 'like' – as central indicators for social and cultural analysis. Affect is often (although not solely) associated with questions of *judgement*, a way of positioning ourselves in relation to others in terms of values and value. Such a starting point must draw from the foundational work of sociologist Pierre Bourdieu whose (1984) *Distinction: A Social Critique of the Judgement of Taste* provides some of the key tools for considering the relations between tastes and social formations. Bourdieu uses an economistic model of taste in which he suggests that taste can operate like an economy in determining social hierarchies. He discusses the operation of 'cultural capital' as central to the way in which social distinctions of class are made and reproduced.

Capitals can be accumulated and accrue value to the individual by having the 'right' taste, moving in the 'right' social circles (social capital) or displaying the 'right' styles (symbolic capital). Our overall composition of these capitals influences the kind of taste judgements that we make and the spaces in which we can operate in a society,

88 FEEL

which helps to produce the social distinctions of class that reach beyond, and help to cement, inequalities that we might have assumed were produced by wealth alone. His concern as a sociologist was with how we learn to live with structures of social differentiation. This references the classic sociological 'structure' versus 'agency' debate in terms of the operation of power whereby the structure refers to the overarching patterns which limit the choices and opportunities available, whilst agency refers to the individual's freedom to act and make choices within those structures. Bourdieu's work asks us to question how power works within particular 'fields' which help to structure these social differences, but then also how we learn to live within, and are constrained or enabled by, these fields in terms of our learned 'habitus' – literally how our bodies move within fields of power. He calls 'habitus' 'history turned into nature' – it is the way in which social positions become operationalised and lived (Bourdieu, 1977: 78).

Cultural capital then can reside in various states – in the institutionalised state (education, art organisations, etc.), the embodied state (language, deportment and style) and in the objectified state (in material goods, possessions and so forth). These forms help to sustain domination and subordination because taste operates as a form of capital – one that can be mobilised and 'traded in' or 'traded up' for educational qualifications, positions in seats of power, spaces in the 'right' circles and so on. For Bourdieu, it is therefore possible to think of a 'cultural economy' one through which the space of culture becomes closely connected to unequal structural social formations. His work has been central to the development of the sociology of consumption and, whilst debates continue about his perhaps overly economistic model and the lack of attention to gender and other social distinctions, his work has still been formative to the analyses of practices of consumption which are in turn useful for media audience research.

It is possible to see how popular media as both content and material artefacts are bound-up within taste cultures of social differentiation. Reapplying Bourdieu's original analysis in a survey into twenty-first century Britain, Bennett et al. (2009) see enduring patterns of taste by occupation and class, with more 'omnivorous' tastes by the middle classes, and more home-centred and community tastes based on fun and entertainment dominating working-class tastes. In this study age, gender and ethnicity were taken more into account; the findings

FEEL 89

echoed older observations from media studies in which women preferred more person-centred narratives (romance films and soap opera) and men generally preferred more 'outward facing' forms such as documentary and sports (Morley, 1986). These categories may seem a little reductive now, given the complexities of consumption presented through convergence culture and they seem to run up against some of the post-structuralist debates about how audience research might reinforce essentialising ideas about gender (Ang and Hermes, 1996; Gauntlett and Hill, 1999).

My own concerns have been with genre that are most often placed at the bottom of hierarchies of gendered and classed models of taste – in my case, I have mostly focussed on TV talk shows and reality television. I would argue that the relations between media and gender must still play a role in any audience analysis even as we are aware that these categories do not necessarily map onto the category of woman in any easy way. Audience research such as my own (Wood and Skeggs, 2012), whilst we struggled against essentialism and reductivism, suggests that we do still need to think about the categories related to class, race, gender and sexuality (and perhaps more so than we have previously disability, age, neurodiversity, and other forms of oppression and exclusion). Patterns of the unequal social order are part of how markers of social 'value' play a role in the generation of hierarchies of taste. Following Bourdieu, those hierarchies can then play a fundamental role in the social spaces that people occupy and in the perpetuation of inequalities.

For instance, in audience research, the *denial* of attachments to particular popular forms, has often surfaced. Audiences wanting to distance themselves from appreciating soap opera (Seiter, 1990), was similarly seen found in our research on reality television, as audiences use media forms precisely to draw social distinctions between themselves and others. Our research showed women expressing surprise that their viewing tastes could be categorised as reality television, 'Oh Goodness, I am watching reality TV' (Skeggs, Thumim and Wood, 2008). Jonathan Gray (2021) argues for a more sustained analysis of dislike alongside audience research into taste and fandom. He reminds us that any analysis of what matters to audiences in terms of passion, commitment and love is incomplete without also attending to 'dislike, alienation, displeasure, annoyance and anger' – for Gray these affects

90 FEEL

too are tightly bound to feelings of belonging and/or alienation in questions of community and identity. Any expression of love towards an object is often also responded to by anti-fan discourse (Gray, 2005) where these feelings are a 'rich site both for feeling the tremors and the after effects of the political realm' (Gray, 2021: 214). Even in relation to the K-Pop phenomena this remains the case, especially as K-Pop sometimes uneasily travels national boundaries and cultural contexts especially in relation to Nationalism and homophobia. In Alptekin and Mutlu's (2021) research on the hashtag #banKpop in Turkey, they discuss the way the anti-fan discourse is mobilised around K-pop's threat to hegemonic masculinity, cuing us in to the 'political tremors' of the contemporary gender order in Turkey. Sociological questions of taste, whilst originally oriented around class, can allow us a way into understanding how affective attachments are important clues into understand the socio-political conjunctural context.

FAN CULTURES AND THE SYMBOLIC POWER OF THE EMOTIONAL REALM

Taste cultures then give us insights into the relations between 'structure' and 'agency', terms derived from sociology to account for the relationship between the governing structure, over which we have relatively little personal control, and the realm of lived experience where we might begin to exercise some autonomy. Certain traditions in the 'active audience' tradition (Chapter 3) have tended to use audience analysis to capture a sense of 'agency' in lived experience over and against 'effects' traditions which assumed that audiences could be easily manipulated (Chapter 2). The 'active audience' tradition was particularly influenced by the work of John Fiske, who saw a good deal of 'symbolic warfare' in audience engagements over any settled account of symbolic hierarchy as determined by texts (Fiske, 1989). Whilst John Fiske was often criticised for being over-celebratory of audience potential by those mostly concerned with political economy and the concentration of media ownership (McChesney, 1996) (Chapter 3), there has since been a revisiting of the tension between political economy and Cultural Studies. In Aniko Bodroghkozy and Henry Jenkins' debate in the journal *Flow* (2005), Jenkins makes it clear that any 'resistant reading was always a survival mechanism in

FEEL 91

a world where media control rested elsewhere, a bottom-up tactic in the face of top-down ideological power.' (2005 online). See Fiske and Hancock's updated (2016) book *Media Matters* which developed a complex account of the struggles between structure and agency in the way media events shape the social landscape. For Jenkins the potential of participatory culture follows Fiske's world 'where consumers and producers confronted each other from positions of unequal power with no guaranteed outcomes, other than the likelihood that both would survive to fight another day' (2005).[3]

The seeds of any radical potential that Jenkins sees in participatory culture (Chapter 1) are directly located within the power of the emotional realm. Fan studies and its concern with intensities of feeling has been committed to the primary questions of how audiences so deeply connect in their attachments to particular media and culture. Henry Jenkins' (1992) formative work in his observations about the story of *The Velveteen Rabbit* (1983), whereby the rabbit becomes real through the love of the adoring child, sets in motion fan studies' concern with how media texts are *made* real and imbued with radical potential, *beyond* any necessary intentions of creators/producer. Rather than seeing audience attachments as infantilising, and part of the picture of 'mass dopes' (Chapter 2), work on fandom has done a great deal to demonstrate the ways in which these relationships should be re-evaluated in terms of their productive potential as part of the more complex set of relations between culture and citizenship (Punathambekar, 2007; Sandvoss, 2012; De Kosnik, 2018; Hinck, 2019).

Gray, Sandvoss and Harrington (2007) describe a first phase of fan studies, as the 'Fandom is beautiful' phase through which a number of scholars actively drew out the cultural production of fans and their challenge to mainstream readings (Bacon-Smith, 1992; Jenkins, 1992; Lewis, 1992; Penley, 1992). Whilst Henry Jenkins' now canonical text *Textual Poachers* drew on Bourdieu, he saw little space within Bourdieu's framework for agency and for the ways in which people operate and 'make do' on the ground. Rather Jenkins utilises Michel De Certeau (1984), who sees various tactics through which people demonstrate their agency daily in practices of consumption. Jenkins' analysis of fans as 'textual poachers', borrowing direct terms from De Certeau, saw their close attachments to television series such as *Star Trek* in their commitment to making their own fan cultural artefacts.

92   FEEL

Fans making zines to centre their preferred narratives or making slash fiction to manage their libidinal desires, positions fans emotional attachments as *productive* and *creative* engagements in contradistinction to the Othering and pathologising narrative of the dopes or misfits of mainstream discourse.

Other work in fandom has focussed on the relationship between 'inner' and 'outer' worlds and the relations between media objects and the formation of subjectivity. This has drawn more on psychoanalytical frameworks than those supported by sociology. Work on stardom and celebrity has used Kleinian approaches (to make the unconscious conscious) to explore the projection and introjection of personal attachments onto objects of desire (Stacey, 1994; Harrisson and Bielby, 1995). For an important account of the benefits and drawbacks of some of this research in the 1990s, see Matt Hills' (2002) *Fan Cultures*. There he outlines a Winnicottian inspired object-relations theory that he suggests can overcome some of the problematic assumptions embedded within fan studies research over moral distinctions, such as the bad object/ good fan, which end up determining fan activities as only compensatory practices for broader social failings (much like other applications of Bourdieu). He suggests that Winnicott offers us the potential to understand how we use media as 'transitional objects' where our inner and outer worlds can be negotiated. This leaves space for some creative agency or 'affective play' without the overdetermining constructivist approach derived from more sociological accounts.

Fan activity and fan production has lauded the potential for generating alternative communities where mainstream texts become resources through which to create strong senses of belonging based on collective forms of fan knowledge. Here, Pierre Bourdieu's work has again been deployed to consider how fan communities themselves generate new forms of cultural capital which create internal hierarchies in a similar economistic mode found in Bourdieu – leading to terms like 'popular cultural capital' (Fiske, 1989) or 'sub-cultural capital' (Thornton, 1995). Indeed a good deal of the debate about fan investments has dovetailed with arguments about the implicit judgements inherent in fan hierarchies, not only between fans, but also between scholars when discussing their own attachments and investments in the kinds of cultural products under study and associations with forms of 'quality' and 'complexity' in cultural artefacts (see Hills, 2002, 2007).

The radical potential of fan communities lies in their ability to generate new forms of cultural exchange and value that are often removed from any economic drive, but are often associated more with 'gift' economies where fans invest time and effort for the love of their cultural attachments and for the communities that grow up around them. For instance, we can look to the many spaces associated with LGBTQ+ fandom precisely because the mainstream excluded their desires (e.g. Mattia, 2018; Guo and Evans 2020; Kuo et al., 2020; McInroy, Zapcic, and Beer, 2022). It is easy to see this exciting potential, but this is also visible to producers and corporations as fan activities and practises have often been appropriated as part of fan management strategies for branding and marketing. Paul Booth (2016) discusses the ways fans operate in a digi-gratis economy whereby there is an interplay between the commercial and gift-economy of fan labours, as they have traditionally given away their fan work for exchange as part of a labour of love. Given the role of this in 'affective economies', Mel Stanfill (2019) refers to this as 'lovebor' as freely given fan work begins to funnel capital back to those concentrated number of key media organisations identified by political economists. I will develop an account of the relationship between affect and labour in Chapter 5 on work, but for now I want to return to the earlier accounts of the way in which emotion generates value in the relations *between* bodies – to explore its relationship to feminist audience research.

THE VALUE OF EMOTION IN FEMINIST AUDIENCE RESEARCH

Feminist audience work on women and soap operas in the 1980s and 1990s operated to intervene in struggles over value whereby wider cultural narratives devalued the object of soap opera and characterised its fans as dopes who were tricked by simplified and overly emotive narratives. In their reappraisal of soap opera consumption, feminist scholars assert the emotive value of soap opera and its space within everyday life as central to understanding its relationship to broader structures of power and patriarchy and in valuing the feminine world of 'emotional realism' (Ang, 1982; Hobson 1980).

94 FEEL

Ien Ang (1982), in her important work on women viewers of the American soap opera *Dallas*,[4] outlines how viewers' attachments were made through an adoption of a 'melodramatic imagination' and a particular 'tragic' 'structure of feeling'. This focus on 'emotional realism' spoke directly to the unhelpful separation of the spheres of realism and emotion and an associated mind and body distinction which has plagued any analysis of mass and popular culture, because it is bound up with one of the most powerful and gendered binaries of Western thought (Huyssen, 1985). It is part of a patriarchal insistence of maintaining the distinction between rationality, objectivity and the public as the legitimate source of authority, whilst relegating the emotional, the subjective and the private to a domestic space without power. Ang's work helped to show how emotional attachments were precisely tied to women's social location in the world – in the valorisation of their knowledge and capacities of the emotional realm. Whilst *Dallas* (and its celebration of a rich elite based around patriarchal oil magnets) might be problematic for feminism as a text – the pleasures that were involved in its viewing needed to be seriously taken into account. Similarly, Purnima Mankekar's (1999) work on Indian television, made a case for the way in which her women viewers channelled a kind of 'symbolic excess' which allowed them to reach into the personal realm, using the personally evocative to understand the growing violence of the Indian state and women's position with its patriarchal nationalism. Feminist audience work therefore has long-challenged an understanding of any separation of emotion from reason and any associated gendered hierarchy between the two.

Such debates have resurfaced in arguments about the power of emotion in the contemporary political sphere, exacerbated by the online environment, and to which I will return (e.g. Wahl-Jorgensen, 2019). I deliberately include this older feminist work here in order to demonstrate that these newer challenges brought by the digital sphere are developments that require us to revisit debates that have long been central to feminist political thought. Nancy Fraser's (1992) critique of Jurgen Habermas' masculinised public sphere' (which has played such a central role in the formation of media studies as a discipline) calls out his vision of an ideal democratic forum because it excludes women and minorities from the terms of debate. Undoing binaries of reason and emotion have always been at the centre of Cultural Studies,

FEEL   95

as Raymond Williams told us ordinary culture is 'not feeling against thought, but thought as felt and feeling as thought' (1977: 32). These works precede the most recent 'affective' turn in the social sciences and it is important to remind us of this as we consider any such 'turn' to affect in media studies.

THE 'AFFECTIVE TURN'

The so-called 'turn' to affect therefore is actually rather a messy one which is influenced by a number of traditions, for instance, there are much longer histories of the psychoanalytic dimensions of emotions (Cvetkovich, 1992), and feminist work on the relationships between women's emotional labour and political structure (Hochchild, 1983). For a really helpful discussion of some of the tensions and limitations of some of these competing traditions as they interface with fields like psychobiology, see Margie Wetherall (2012). The 'affective turn' (Clough and Halley, 2007) of the late 1990s and 2000s appeared in cultural theory in part as a response to what was seen as broader cultural shifts in the political landscape. As we have already seen, none of the approaches to 'knowing' audiences that we have discussed thus far in this book (see Chapter 2), are free from the social contexts in which they have been produced, and the affective turn in the social sciences is the same. In the mid-90s cultural commentators began to discuss a re-framing of the political realm as part of the new re-ordering of public life, where changes in citizenship meant greater claims to personal victimhood and appeals to individual feelings seemed to flood the cultural and political landscape political realm. Lauren Berlant (1997) refers to this in the context of American culture as an 'intimate public sphere' – one where individualised claims to sentiment that were once part of the private realm become part of a more widespread individualising of nationhood and a re-investment in normative ideals of family and of personal life.

Broader accounts from cultural theory seemed to suggest some larger psychic affects, at the level of national and even global scale. Some come as the product of the analysis of late capitalism's neoliberal appeals to the investment in 'the self' as consumerism drew from the very repertoires of feminism and the appeals to make the 'personal political' (Gill, 2007; McRobbie, 2008). This positioned emotional life at the centre of public, political and commercial

96 FEEL

discourse. These type of stories of 'personal journeys' abound in the self-help industry and in television and lifestyle narratives (White, 1992; Weber, 2009). Such narratives also help to serve an ideological imperative to expel communitarian ideals of the social contract and support for welfare provision and replace them with appeals for individualised introspection and personal effort (Ouellette and Hay, 2008). At the same time, as narratives of personal victimhood abound, the post-colonial landscape engenders powerful affects in response to shifting national boundaries, which include the rise of nationalist sentiments and right-wing populist fervour (Chouliaraki and Banet-Weiser, 2021). Paul Gilroy refers to a sentiment in the British context as a 'post-imperial melancholia' (2004) where the nation has not moved on from its Imperial past and is struggling to cope with a sense of loss. But for audience studies these 'affective moods' need testing on ground at the interface of psychological explanation and Media and Cultural Studies (Blackman and Walkerdine, 2001).

What is curious though is that the 'affective turn' in cultural theory has rarely directly engaged with the histories of fan research, or with earlier feminist audience research where the territory of overlapping tensions between biological and cultural responses has been extensively explored, if not, of course, resolved. One reason might be that when media and cultural theorists took up this new mantel, they did so by suggesting a break with questions of representation that had previously dominated much of mainstream Media and Cultural Studies (see Chapter 3). As we discussed in the last chapter, understanding the workings of ideology drew heavily on European traditions of semiology – the analysis of sign systems and the politics of representation. Then later it drew its energy from the analysis of discourse (the production of knowledge as established through an episteme) as influenced by the work of Michel Foucault in the broader post-structuralist turn to deconstruction. The idea that has held sway in some appeals for an 'affective turn' is that it occurs in opposition to, and outside of, the more restrictive realm of social construction and social determinism.

This position was most prominently observed in Brian Massumi's (2002) *Parables for the Virtual* in which he laments the ways that critical thinking's attention to the discursive realm becomes trapped in an endless cycle of being able to prove that which it sets out to find. His

FEEL 97

argument to put bodies back into critical theory is an optimistic one, and is done in order to be able to account for the movements of thought and feelings and their relationship to change, which deconstructivism seems unable to capture. Following Deleuze (1997), Massumi focusses instead on the affective as a state of being which is in a constant process of 'becoming' and therefore more useful to the cultural theorist for its radical potential. This does indeed seem persuasive and it separates out the affective bodily reactions and their unpredictable potential from the ways in which the cultural determinants of feelings are coded and frozen in the discursive realm.

This attention to 'affect', as distinct from feeling or emotion, offers us a clear separation of these fields: 'emotion refers to cultural and social expression whereas affects are of a biological and physiological nature' (Probyn, 2005: 11). For Sianne Ngai (2005) on the other hand such a bifurcation is unhelpful since that distinction itself is bound up with the psychoanalytic problem it was designed to solve and she uses the terms interchangeably. Insisting on such a clear distinction between 'emotion' and 'affect' however presents a particular problem for audience studies, which I will explain. In Claire Hemming's (2005) critique of Massumi (and of Eve Sedgewick) she is troubled by the way such a bifurcation also sets up another problematic dyadic - between so called 'affective freedom' (of the body) and the restricted 'social determinism' (of the social order). As Hemmings points out and as we can see in the writings of postcolonial and critical race theory (e.g. Spivak, 1993; Bhabha, 1994; Hill Collins, 2000) affect can just as easily play a role in cementing sexed and raced realms of domination, as much as it might have the seeds for sowing some optimistic potential for change.

To propose an 'affective-turn' that refutes 'meaning-making' seems rather counter-intuitive for an audience studies informed by Cultural Studies where meaning has been a fundamental object of study for the field. Should accounts of 'non-representational theory' – that have drawn from cultural geography and the work of scholars such as Nigel Thrift (2007) which refer to affective states, atmospheres, the bodily and the sensory – suggest a total move beyond 'meaning'? Ruth Leys (2017) for instance is critical of the ways in which some of the theories of affect seem to embed an anti-intentionalism as though there is no power or force behind some of the workings of affect. Whilst Mark

98 FEEL

Andrejevic (2013) points to a strange synergy between marketeers' popularisation of consumer behaviour and emerging theories of affect 'taken up by writers normally considered to be critical' (2013: 155–156). Scholars have of course pointed to the political mobilisation of affect, most notably Sarah Ahmed's work on 'affective economies' which refers to the currency of how negative feelings 'stick' to some bodies more than others in the perpetuation of inequalities. (Ahmed, 2004). For instance, using textual research, Imogen Tyler (2008) has shown us the mobilisation of classed disgust in the images of the 'chav mum' in the UK, whilst I have traced the movement of online affect into the realms of classed digital contagion in the case of the shaming of the 'Magaluf Girl' (Wood, 2018).

Given this history, it is not surprising that the analysis of affect has had more impact in the development of media theory than it has to empirical audience studies (Gibbs, 2011). Work has often drawn out theoretical abstract accounts of the work of media images in the generating and circulation of fear (Massumi, 1993, 2005; Gibbs, 2007, 2008) than on testing out how affective practices might operate in lived experience. But we can begin to see a way forward for empirical audience research. For instance, Kristyn Gorton's (2009) book offers us an excellent account of the multiple ways in which television as a form generates emotional attachments with audiences, drawing together the literature around the 'affective turn' with longer histories from fan and media audience research.

To conduct audience analysis, we can draw upon Margie Wetherall's (2012) work which wholly takes issue with the idea that the affective turn must insist on a 'rubbishing of discourse' and argues for a more integrated understanding of the relationships between discourses and bodily actions, suggesting the formulation of 'affective practice'. 'An affective practice is a figuration where body possibilities and routines become recruited or entangled together with meaning-making and with other social and material figurations' (2014: 19). This approach seems to me to be more in line with early Cultural Studies' signposting of the relationship between affective states and social dynamics that were set in motion in Williams' early observations about 'structures of feeling'. Andre Cavalcante (2018) argues that we need analyses of affect to complement our understanding of ideological interpretations. They show how LGBTQ+ audiences also need to incorporate rest and

FEEL   99

resilience to cope with some of the demands that audiencing takes as a more dynamic and embodied experience. Such an approach therefore has the capacity to respond to the need for an expanded repertoire to account for the overlapping layers of meaning in our analysis, that we discussed in Chapter 3.

TESTING AMBIGUITIES

One way in which the analysis of affect becomes very useful in audience research is in the analysis of ambiguity. A common finding in audience research is that the results are ambiguous – audience responses are rarely stable and they often show up contradictory insights. But it is important to interrogate that ambiguity for what those tensions tell us 'about everything else'. Beverley Skeggs and I have argued that affect is not entirely unknowable and structureless, just because it is unstable and unpredictable, else why do so many affective drives seem to confirm expected formations of normativity and domination as much as, if not even more so, than they upset them? (Skeggs and Wood, 2012). We also took our cue from Deleuze's reading of Spinoza who used affects to explore the working of power exercised by sixteenth-century priests over their congregation (Deleuze and Deleuze, 1978). Spinoza's theory of affect draws on what he calls the 'force of existing' which can be in variance and unstable in multiple social encounters – when we come into contact with others power works through affect to enhance or diminish our capacity to act. If we think back to the opening of this chapter, where we discussed Bourdieu's ideas of 'capitals' and 'values' to help explain inequalities, it is possible to think about the way in which certain forms of cultural capital for instance might make us 'feel', and how power can operate on the ground in and through interactions and experiences. As Beverley Skeggs (2004: 89) points out: 'affect may enable us to explore how use-values are experienced, expressed and known'. Think about the ways in which feelings of (not) belonging in certain social spaces and situations where unspoken peri-performances of shame can be embodied and transmitted through the glance or the look – and how these can be deeply *felt*.

These ideas can be useful for audience research because it allows us a way out of the binary way of thinking that has dominated an

100 FEEL

approach (often located within semiotics) and drawn out in active audience theory and sometimes in fan studies, of the 'bad' text versus the 'good' audience – as though each of those entities were entirely stable. Lawrence Grossberg (1997, 2010) has argued that affect is the 'missing link' in the persistent puzzle over the relationship between understanding media messages and ideology. Feminist scholars have long been testing these waters, asking how can we explain women's attachments to texts that are apparently ideologically 'bad' for them? How do the questions of pleasure and attachments, saturated in our broader relational and emotional histories, offer meanings that work around, just as they re-embed, the systems that are meant to oppress us? Melanie Kennedy, Jilly Kay and I (2019), for instance have argued for a serious revisiting of pleasure in attachments to the contemporary wedding spectacle *precisely because* they come at the same time that marriage is deemed less necessary within the gender order. The freedom/domination dialectic has never been straight forward in almost any audience research generated from a Cultural Studies point of view and it begets the audience researcher to do the work of deciphering this complexity, of testing out how alternative affective states can co-exist, exactly to be more precise about any easy bifurcation between 'affective freedom' and 'social domination'.

REACTING TO REALITY TELEVISION: AUDIENCE, AFFECTS AND THE SOCIAL REALM

The phrase 'affective economies' currently gets used fairly liberally in media research, because obviously that is what the media industries are working with – the capacity to generate all manner of intrigue, joy, pleasure, excitement and turn them into economic profit. In our work on reality television we could see how the huge profits of the television industries were drawn from an arena through which 'ordinary' participants were called to generate emotion and feeling – acting, up, breaking down, falling out – (mostly for free) across our screens as this new conjunctural moment of intense public intimacy was lucratively exploited. What concerned us at the time was how these performances seemed to outline a particular way of understanding new class formations within neoliberal culture. We argued that across many reality television texts those participants who understood the

FEEL **101**

codes of self-work and self-transformation faired better than those that did not. Those deemed to be failing in these performances of emotion offered the most to a television narrative of self-development, but most importantly, this was contributing to a new way of 'seeing' the working class as 'failing' individual subjects through stories and codes which refused any broader social explanation of the conditions of their existence. Of course ideological scripts like this do not simply appear from nowhere and we argued that they are a product of longer histories of the ways in which the calculation of personhood (in relation to education, taste, lifestyle, etc.) are some of the very central tenets of the project of the bourgeoise subject before neoliberalism. It seemed as though reality television in the UK, especially in its Pygmalion narratives and its generation of competing class conflict, was playing out a new 'spectacular morality' that was reinventing class in the political landscape. (Wood and Skeggs, 2008)

In our audience research project *Reacting to Reality Television*[5] (Skeggs and Wood, 2012) we wanted to try to understand what this meant in terms of class formation for viewers. How did they react and respond to all of this emotion on screen as it seemed to replay some of the dominant ideological scripts of that socio-political conjuncture? One of the remarkable things about reality television's *form,* its manipulation of immediacy and intimacy, is that not all moments, even as they are edited to televisual narrative conventions, are entirely predictable. Reality television, in capturing unscripted performances allowed for moments of unpredictable rupture within episodes and series – and for some critics lots of reality television defied any ideological purity (Kavka, 2008). The 'bad text' argument and any representational certainties were difficult to pin down securely.

Our audience study involved 40 women from four different socially located groups across London, who took part in three different stages of audience research – this included interviews, 'text-in-action' sessions (as described in Chapter 3) where we recorded viewers responses to reality television in time allowing us to access some of these 'moments' of television, as well as focus groups. We found that there were precise 'moments' where some of the symbolic codes of texts which we called 'judgement shots' (for instance shots of excessive food, messy homes, images of smoking, drinking), would align with audiences' immediate affective reactions – tuts, gasps, sighs. These immediate reactions were then often converted into more discursive forms of moral judgement, 'how can they do that?' 'oh my goodness how awful' in ways in which we might have predicted given the nature of the editing (often juxtaposing 'good' behaviour against 'bad' for instance). The research often mirrored other contemporaneous research around reality television audiences (Hill, 2005, 2007; Sender, 2012) in which the pedagogic lessons of reality television found some traction and through which audiences accessed *Shadenfreude* in order to feel relieved at their own personal circumstances – 'thank goodness my life is not like that'.

Yet the space we created through our methods for affective resonances also allowed us to see how affect can tell us something of other affects that resonated across the findings. As well as judgement, we also found a good deal of empathy and care, where audiences would 'reach through' the coding of the text to find common ground with those on the screen. Judgement and empathy could co-exist and certainly did not fall into neat class lines where we might expect middle-class participants to assume a viewing position of superiority, as some of the literature born from textual analysis had claimed. Rather our audience research demonstrated a more complex interweaving of experiences and emotion related to social locations, experiences and sites where class intersects with gender and race – a complexity that mirrors David Morley's (1980) earlier attempt to map social location and reading positions discussed in Chapter 3.

What we did find was a fairly reliable 'affective practice', to borrow with hindsight from Wetherell's later formulation, 'where body possibilities and routines become recruited or entangled together with meaning making and with other social and material figurations' (2012: 19). Whilst there was a good deal of movement between empathy and judgement in different moments of television viewing, where we did see social patterns was in the ways in which our audiences could draw on their own capitals and sources of value to resource those judgements – to convert their affective reactions into some form of moral authority. Our South Asian viewers from Clapham drew on relationships related to cultural difference; our middle-class viewers from Forest Hill drew upon their cultural and educational capitals and could operationalise a certain distance from the text more easily; whilst our working-class participants from Addington (mostly white) and Brockley (of mixed races) drew on their capacities for 'good' motherhood.

Drawing attention to those audience reactions that displayed the most intensity of feeling in our research, helped to demonstrate the work that affect can do in the formation of power relationships between people. When watching the TV programme *Wife Swap* (in which two wives swapped placed for two weeks, trying on the others' lifestyle) the most virulent and animated reactions came from working-class mothers dealing with similar battles in relation to working lives and motherhood (Figure 4.1: Sal and Sonia watch *Wife Swap* Channel 4).

Sal and Sonia, in the extract from our data below, begin to act out what is happening on the screen, as was common when audiences felt a particular proximity with the issues at hand. Later work by Lunenborg and Maier (2019) used video recordings to record reactions to the television screen and showed how reality television audiences in 'sharing the excitement' (2019: 152) mimic actions and even in some cases anticipate them, such is the intensity of affect travelling between bodies on screen and bodies in the home.

In our audience research data, the most powerful reactions convert into some form of strong moral vitriol or anger were from our working-class mothers towards more aspirational and seemingly 'un-caring' mothers on screen as we can see in the extract below. As Sara Ahmed (2004) and Skeggs (2004) argue, emotions work to align subjects with and against others, which is why they have such powerful political force. During the text-in-action viewing session, Sonia tells us that she is also a legal secretary like the woman on screen and has made difficult choices around work and motherhood. The emotional investment that she makes here relates to the way in which television participants de/legitimate the choices and values of viewers. In work on affect, both Ahmed (2004) and Probyn (2004) suggest that there must be some contact or threat of contact in order for disgust, and the pulling away it involves, to take place. In our analysis of this particular affective resonance around mothering, we must also understand that discursively the notion of the 'good mother' has become such a dominant trope in the surveillance and evaluation of working-class women (Lawler, 2000). This is an environment where competitive mothering has thrived in neoliberal culture (Jensen, 2018) so much that its presence becomes such a powerful political mark of association and alignment through

104 FEEL

Audio marker Visual Image	Programme audio extract Wife Swap	Viewers' comments
1	18:19		
2	Image of car	**Voice over**: Unfamiliar with the	
3	clock	journey from Manchester	
4		its taking Kate	
5	Kate driving	<u>long</u>er than expected to get ho:me which only <u>adds</u> to her	
6		frustration.	
7	Kate to camera		
8	whilst driving	**Kate:** I <u>ca:n't</u> belie::ve it's eight	**Sally**: Nightmare, absolute
9		o'clock and I left home <u>thir</u>teen ho:urs ago (1) I've- no wonder	nightmare in it?
10	Kate pulling onto	I've got a headache its just	
11	drive	ri<u>di</u>culous	
12			**Sonia:** I had to leave home at seven
13		**Voice over:** By the time Kate	with (?child's name) to get to work
14	Kate enters the	gets ho:me its <u>eigh</u>t thirty.	and drop them off I had to leave at
	house / Lottie		seven
15	sleeeping	**Kate**: How's Lottie?	
16		**Mark**: She:'s <u>fast</u> asleep in bed (.)	
17		**Kate:** ah	
18		**Mark**: she's <u>shatt</u>ered	
	Kate to Camera	**Kate**: Ah:::	
		Kate: [whispering to camera] I':m quite disappointed that	**Sally:** Oh <u>no:</u> she's cry:ing, she's having a ↑<u>mare</u> of a day::.
	Lottie sleeping	Lottie was in bed and I didn't get to bath her	**All:** Yeah.
	Kate and Mark in the living room	I'm <u>so</u> tired	**Sonia**: She's not had her all day really has she? I suppose with all
		Kate: My <u>bod</u>y feels re:ally ali:ve but my head feels dead .hh	them children ((?))

Figure 4.1 Brockley is a ward of Lewisham in South London that is characterised by a larger than average African and Caribbean population and social by housing.[6]

FEEL 105

Cut to other family	quite often at home it's the other way round. Hh hh	**Sal:** But (its alright but) that's not fair on that child!
	Mark: Do you think Tracy would be feeling like that now?	**Sonia**: Exa:ctly and that's what she's feelin'
		Sal: ((?))
		Sonia: mmm I'm taking the mother's role **[performs]** and when I wo:ke you up and dragged you out of bed at six o'clock in the morning [and dropped you off at seven o'clock
		Sal: [to have you out by seven
		Sonia: and now its eight thirty at night and you ain't seen me all day::::.
		Sal: The kid's in ↑bed.
		Sonia: How you gonna make up for that?
		Sal: You ca::n't
		(6)

Figure 4.1 Continued

which the women from our audiences tried to display their proximity, precisely when the narrative on screen, we might say 'touched a nerve', in its proximity to their own lives. Here, 'affective economies' as distributed across social fields in the way Ahmed (2004) describes, directly relate to the ideological terrain which attaches value to mothering through wider cultural discourses.

We use such examples to suggest that the affective practices we can see here across our data are engagements in 'tournaments of value' – responding to the broader political rise of cultures of measurement and evaluation of the self in neoliberalism that have been part of a longer project of the formation of the bourgeois subject. The affective intensities of audience responses sometimes replay ideological scripts, but also offer up moments of ambiguity and circumvention that are more deeply rooted in complex affective registers revealing of the cultural conjuncture in a way reminiscent of Raymond Williams' original intention. From this evidence, we understand that all of our viewers were always engaging in value struggles such that by, 'mapping failure and lack of value reality television incited our audiences to defend and prove their own, and in this reaction their investment in the ideological mechanism of value struggle itself was secured' (Skeggs and Wood, 2012: 233).

I use this example because a focus on how affect works (and the willingness to use alternative methods outside of the interview and the focus group) can be productive for audience studies. Sara de Beneditis (2017) also uses this method to show how audiences negotiate the terms of a good birth in *One Born Every Minute* (Channel4 2010–) drawing out the visceral experiences of labour. It offers us ways of capturing intensities and proximities and is able to test some of the assumptions made about broader political and national sentiments (see also Coleman and Ross, 2010). This kind of approach, capturing affective processes empirically with audiences allows us to 'see' affect at work.

AUDIENCE, SOCIAL MEDIA AND CONTAGION

Thus far in this chapter, I have tried to account for some trajectories of audience research which address similar questions about the importance of feeling to audience analysis. Affect studies have found fertile soil in social media analyses, largely because networked media provides the technical ground for ideas, feelings and emotions to spread with ease often conjuring biological metaphors of contagion and virality. Greg Seigworth (2018) in the foreword to the text *Affect and Social Media* draws on Gilles Deleuze's (1995) observation about control societies – that it is easy 'to set up a correspondence between any society and some kind of machine'. Seigworth goes on, 'That dimly emergent structure of feeling that Deleuze intuited almost thirty years ago now is our dominant infrastructure of affective inter-relation' (2018: xii). The presence of 'emoticons' and the way in which they 'fix' the emotional complexity of the user is perhaps emblematic of a growing and entwined relationship between feelings and technological affordances (Ellis, 2018).

Some of the major concerns of the power of social media have been about the ways in which it can be used and manipulated to sway public opinion and generate feelings of political intensity that may then have particular effects. Recent examples include the Facebook's Cambridge Analytica scandal and the profiling of user data in order to help sway the Brexit vote.[7] Such mechanisms allow for an analysis of the ways in which social media can trigger mass contagion, referencing the older work of Gabriel Tarde, which extends the ways in which social psychologists have long been concerned with the spread of moods and feelings (and unrest) as discussed in Chapter 2 around audience histories.

Studies of social media use have therefore been concerned with platforms' ability to ignite and mobilise particular, often politicised sentiment. The work of Zizi Papacharizzi (2014) calls these 'affective publics' in the analysis of the Twitter mobilisations of the Occupy movement, the Arab Spring, and of the #Thisisacoup hashtags in Greece. Here the ways in which virality takes hold can carry huge political potential generating, 'networked public formations that are mobilized and connected or disconnected through expressions of sentiment' (2014: 125). We might be able to think of any other number of similar movements from #MeToo, the feminist anti-sexual violence movement, or the #BringBackOurGirls action which advocates for the return of the abducted Chibok schoolgirls in Nigeria, bringing the case to international prominence. There are a number of high-profile luminous cases whereby the mediation of citizen-feelings has been profoundly bound-up with political change, however, Papacharizzi is also keen to point out that affective publics support connective, but not necessarily collective, action. This is similar to Jodi Dean's (2005) cautions about 'communicative capitalism' which is communication geared to profit over democracy.

But the visibility of discussion on social media platforms like X/Twitter now give the analyst a way to measure and assess public/ audience opinions in hitherto unreachable numbers, and as a result there has been a turn to the 'quantification' of feelings and sentiment in order to guage the cultural 'mood' or zeitgeist. In fan studies Gray Sandvoss and C. Lee Harrington (2017) describe a third wave of the field whereby social media makes fan studies increasingly important to these questions about the generation of affective communities in political discussions. Audience feeling in relation to the political (with a capital P), can now be discerned in the 'fanisation' of political movements, propelled by participatory culture whereby populist sentiment relies on antagonistic relationships. We can see how fan and anti-fan dynamics supported the rise of AltRight and the popularity of a President like Donald Trump, or lend themselves easily to K-Pop's political activism with which we opened this chapter.

One of the key differences now is one of method - through social media we can read the engagements of television texts in real time in X/Twitter feeds to gauge the sentiment and feelings of an audience. For example, Dayna Chatman (2017) discusses the fan and anti-fan Twitter articulations of Black women responding to Shonda Rhimes' major ABC TV series *Scandal* (significant as a major networked series with a Black woman as the lead). The emerging heated discussion of respectability politics of Black women as the 'side-chick' (a woman who steals another woman's man), allows Chatman to argue that, 'The Black fan and anti-fan online struggle over representations of black women on television should not be dismissed as politically inconsequential, but rather must be situated along a continuum of practices of ideological development which serve as the building blocks for political consciousness and action' (2017: 313).

The interrogation of 'affective communities' are the heart of social media studies just, as they have been at the heart of audience studies born out of Cultural Studies' attention to 'structures of feeling'. Traditional audience studies and some social media analysis have a good deal in common, and it is striking just how often Raymond Williams' discussion of a 'structure of feeling' comes into play in analyses of internet practices. Perhaps this is because Williams (1961) was exceptionally prescient about the role communication technologies must play in any 'long revolution' – see also Fuchs (2017) – but it is also because of the way in which Williams' sense of a structure of feeling captures the relationship of culture to dynamic change.

For Raymond Williams (1961: 69) a structure of feeling is '…is as firm and as definite as 'structure' suggests, yet it operates in the most intangible parts of our activity.' … 'and what is particularly interesting is that it does not seem to be in any formal sense learned.' In separating out culture in dominant (mainstream), residual (past remnants) and emergent (newly forming) cultures Williams (1977) opens up a way of seeing culture as still in process, as not yet formed, as 'social experiences in solution, as distinct from other social semantic formations which have been less precipitated and are more evidentiary and more immediately available' (1977: 132). We can hear the echoes in Massumi's analysis of the 'not yet' of becoming which has been so very important to the analysis of the immediacy and instantaneity of digital culture. In Papacharissi's work (2015) on the ways in which Twitter users help to construct the story of news events in real time, she relies on Williams to explain the storytelling structures of feelings sustained by spreadable technologies. 'In the same manner, we may understand and further interpret collaborative discourses organized by hashtags on Twitter as structures of feeling, comprising an organically developed pattern of impulses, restraints, and tonality' (2015: 15). This emphasis on 'impulses, restrains and tonality' comes directly from Williams and captures senses of meaning-making beyond the semantic. His emphasis on structures, which explore the interrelationship between *forms* and rhythm to the social order, are useful touch points across all manner of audience engagements in relation to any media.

CONCLUSION

We opened with the question: *What can feelings tell us about media audiences and changing social relations?* This chapter argues that thinking about feelings should be central to a Cultural Studies approach to audience analysis, not only because feelings tell us about personal attachments to media questions of value in the social order. But feelings can also give us insight into the dynamic nature of culture and any potential for changing power relations. Capturing 'emergent' cultural forms is what unites traditional audience research and more contemporary social media analysis. K-Pop is seemingly engendering new global forms of passionate attachments to media objects at the same time that its participatory framework is taking political directions that we could not predict in new formations of cultural citizenship. To be alert to emergent trends is to adopt an understanding of ambivalence and ambiguity as culture comes into being and the dialogues between fan and anti-fan discourse give us some of the most visible markers of these dynamics.

110 FEEL

Audience engagements operate 'in solution' in a 'not yet' space which enables us to track and feel our way through social change as it is lived and experienced. The key point of attending to the specificities of these as 'structures' is to try and mark out their political significance to questions of power. For instance within Ien Ang's (1982) discussion of women viewers of the soap opera *Dallas* and their 'tragic structure of feeling' an adoption of a 'melodramatic imagination' is an emergent cultural form. One which is prophetic of broader shifts in cultural expression that later cultural theorists have called the 'intimate public sphere' (Berlant, 1997). Our work on affective 'tournaments of value' (Skeggs and Wood, 2012) identifies how reality television encourages a personal calibration of ones place in the world which we might see as one of the many signs towards cultures of neoliberalism in which self-evaluation and measurement abound in a move towards 'algorithmic culture' (Striphas, 2015). The point for the audience researcher is in the use of feeling as an analytic tool for what it tells us about everything else – for what it means for the conjunctural moment, that we discussed in Chapter 1.

I have tried in this chapter to draw out some of the through-lines of traditional audience analysis to the contemporary moment because discussion of networked affects and affective publics often take place without these particular histories. Williams has always insisted on the inter-relationship between industry, democracy and culture. The shifting lines of communication across alternative platforms generate new relations between community and communication and these are often framed with new questions of tonality and intensity – new questions of tone and speed – new questions of *form* derived from digital interfaces to which we will return in Chapter 6. Perhaps what is different is the myriad ways in which affective practices derive data capital extraction in what has been described by some as 'affective capitalism' (Karppi et al., 2016). All social media practices rely on a sense of 'audiencing' in the broadest sense from being heard to being seen, to becoming part of an aggregate of numbers for advertising or political opinion. In the contemporary digital context, even more so than in our audience research on reacting to reality television, affective engagements also involve affective *performances* – things we do, make and share in the form of memes, gifs, vlogs and so forth – as part of ordinary experience. These digital affective performances are

FEEL **111**

now available for commodification and make the audience researcher concerned with questions of 'affective labour' – another debate that has often been at the heart of audience studies as the next chapter will go on to explore.

NOTES

1 https://www.vam.ac.uk/articles/k-pop-fandom (accessed May 25, 2023).
2 https://www.nytimes.com/2020/06/21/style/tiktok-trump-rally-tulsa.html (accessed May 25, 2023).
3 https://www.flowjournal.org/2005/06/why-fiske-still-matters/ (accessed May 26, 2023).
4 Dallas was an American prime time television soap opera that aired on CBS from April 2, 1978, to May 3, 1991. The series revolves around an affluent and feuding Texas family, the Ewings, who own the independent oil company Ewing Oil and the cattle-ranching land of Southfork.
5 Funded by the ESRC Identities and Social Action Programme.
6 https://www.nytimes.com/2018/04/04/us/politics/cambridge-analytica-scandal-fallout.html.
7 Area Profile Summary
Our four groups of ten women were recruited from friendship networks from four areas of south London.
The **New Addington** group is all white and working class. Five mothers, five non-mothers, ages 18–72. Occupations mainly centre on care work and full-time mothering. New Addington is a ward of Croydon, an outer London Borough, and is noted for its physical isolation, with a population of 10,351. Nearly one-half of the accommodation of the area is social council rented housing, with an unemployment rate of 4%. It is mostly white (88%) and most of the population, nearly 90%, is born in the UK.
The **Forest Hill** group is middle class working in arts and education, mostly white and mixed race. Seven white, three self-defined as mixed race, all self-defined as middle-class (three mothers, seven non-mothers), ages 30–57. Occupations centre on public sector educational, art and psy-drama work. Forest Hill is a ward of Lewisham, an inner London Borough, with a population of 14,000. Over one-half of the accommodation in the area is owner occupied (Victorian housing) and approximately 23% is council housing with 9% unemployment. It has a 30% population of black or minority ethnic residents, lower than the average for inner London, and just over 70% of its population were born in the UK.
The **Brockley** group is racially mixed, white and Caribbean, and all working class. Six black British, three white, one Maltese (only one not a mother), ages 26–68. Occupations in public sector and service sector administrative, caring and sec-retarial work. Brockley is another ward of Lewisham in inner London with a population of 13,697. Of the housing in this area 37% is owner occupied and 26% council rented, with 8% unemployment. Brockley has a lower percentage of

112 FEEL

British residents (48.8%) than the London average (59.8%), nearly 30% identify themselves as black or black British, mostly Caribbean or African.

The **Clapham** group are Southern and British Asian, Asian, Pakistani, Bangladeshi, settled and recently arrived; transnational class differences, seven mothers, two non-mothers) ages 18–45. Two are highly educated professional women, one student, the rest full-time mothers or part-time helpers with husband's work. Clapham is a ward of Lambeth in inner London with a population of 13,332. Most accommodation in Clapham consists of flats of which approximately 35% are owner occupied, 62% are rented (30% rented from the council), with 4.7% unemployment. Clapham is known to be a rather diverse area in terms of affluence and ethnicity, 38% of the population are from ethnic minorities.

(Area information compiled from 2001 Census: http://neighbourhood.statistics. gov.uk and http://www.ideal-homes.org.uk.)

REFERENCES

Ahmed, S. (2004) 'Affective Economies' *Social Text* 22 (2): 117–139.

Alptekin, K. and Mutlu, B. (2021) 'Anti-K-pop discourse in turkey and the tactical struggle of K-pop fans', *Momentdergi* 8 (1):144–167.

Andrejevik, M. (2013) *Infoglut: How Too Much Information Is Changing the Way We Think and Know.* London: Routledge.

Ang, I. (1982) *Watching Dallas Soap Opera and the Melodramatic Imagination.* London and New York, Routledge.

Ang, I. and Hermes, J. (1996) 'Gender and/in media consumption', in Curran, J. and Gurevitch, M. (eds.) *Mass Media and Society.* London: Edward Arnold, pp. 307–328.

Bennett, T., Savage, M., Silva, E., Gayo-Cal, M., and Wright, D. (2009) *Culture, Class, Distinction.* London and New York: Routledge.

Berlant, L. (1997) *The Queen of American Goes to Washington City: Essays on Sex and Citizenhip* Durham NC: Duke University Press.

Bhabha, H. K. (1994) *The Location of Culture,* London: Routledge.

Blackman, L. and Walkerdine, V. (2001) *Mass Hysteria: Critical Psychology and Media Studies.* Basingtsike: Palgrave.

Booth, P. (2016) *Digital Fandom 2.0: New Media Studies.* Publisher: Bristol, Peter Lang.

Bourdieu, P. (1977) *Outline of a Theory of Practice.* Cambridge: Cambridge University Press.

Bourdieu, P. (1984) *Distinction: A Social Critique of the Judgement of Taste.* London: Routledge and Kegan Paul.

Cavalcante, A. (2018) 'Affect, emotion, and media audiences: The case of resilient reception', *Media, Culture & Society* 40(8): 1186–1201. doi: 10.1177/0163443718781991.

Chatman, D. (2017) '18. Black twitter and the politics of viewing scandal', in Jonathan Gray, Cornel Sandvoss and C. Lee (eds.) *Fandom, Second Edition: Identities and Communities in a Mediated World.* Harrington, NY: New York University Press, pp. 299–314.

FEEL **113**

Chouliaraki, L. and Banet-Weiser, S. (2021) ,Introduction to special issue: The logic of victimhood', *European Journal of Cultural Studies* 24 (1): 3–9.

Clough, P.T. and Halley, J. (2007) *The Affective Turn: Theorising the Social*. Durham and London: Duke University Press.

Coleman, S. and Ross, K. (2010) *The Media and the Public: 'Them and Is' in Media Discourse (Political Communication)*. West Sussex: Wiley-Blackwell.

Cvetkovich, A. (1992) *Mixed Feelings: Feminism, Mass Culture, and Victorian Sensationalism*. New York: Rutgers University Press.

Dean, J. (2005) 'Communicative capitalism: circulation and the foreclosure of politics', *Cultural Politics* 1: 51–74.

De Beneditis, S. (2017) 'Watching one born every minute: negotiating the terms of a good birth', in Moseley, R., Wheatley, H., and Wood, H. (eds.) *Television for Women: New Directions*. London: Routledge, pp. 110–127.

De Certeau, M. (1984) *The Practice of Everyday Life*. Berkeley, CA: University of California Press.

De Kosnik, A. (2018) 'Filipinos forced fandom of US Media: Protests against the Daily Show and Desperate Housewives as bid for cultural citizenship', in Click, M. and Scott, S. (eds.) *Routledge Companion to Media Fandom*. New York: Routledge, pp. 262–270.

Deleuze, G. (1995) 'Postscript on the socities of control', in *Negotiations*. Cambridge, MA: Columbia University Press.

Deleuze, G. (1997) *Essays Critical and Clinical*, trans. D. W. Smith and M. A. Greco. Minneapolis, MN: University of Minnesota Press.

Deleuze, E. and Deleuze, J. (1978) 'Giles Deleuze: Lecture Transcripts on Spinoza's Concept of Affect' Vol 2006 http://www.webdeleuze.com/php/sommaire. html

Ellis, D. (2018) 'Social media, emoticons and process', in Sampson, T., Maddison, S., and Ellis, D. (eds.) *Affect and Social Media*. London and New York: Rowman and Littlefield, pp. 18–25.

Fiske, J. and Hancock, B.H. (2016) *Media matters: Race & gender in US politics*. London and New York, Routledge.

Fiske, J. (1989) *Understanding Popular Culture*. Boston, MA: Unwin Hyman.

Fraser, N. (1992) 'Rethinking the public sphere: A contribution to the critique of actually existing democracy', in Calhoun, C. (ed.) *Habermas and the Public Sphere*. Cambridge, MA: MIT Press, pp 109–142.

Fuchs, C. (2017) 'Raymond Williams' communicative materialism', *European Journal of Cultural Studies* 20 (6): 744–762.

Gauntlett, D. and Hill, A. (1999) *TV Living: Television Culture and Everyday Life*. London: Routledge.

Gibbs, A. (2007) *Horriefied: Embodied Vision, Media Affect and the Images from Abu Graib*. Interrogating the War on Terror, Cambridge: Cambridge Scholars.

Gibbs, A. (2008) 'Cartographies of feeling: one night's tango in Paris', *Emotion, Space and Society* 1 (2): 102–105.

Gibbs, A. (2011) 'Affect theory and audience', in Nightingale, V. *The Handbook of Media Audiences*. Malden, MA: Wiley Blackwell.

114 FEEL

Gill, R. (2007) 'Postfeminist media culture', *European Journal of Cultural Studies* 10 (2): 147–166.

Gilroy, P. (2004) *Postcolonial Melancholia*. New York: Columbia University Press.

Gorton, K. (2009) *Media Audiences: Television, Meaning and Emotion*. Edinburgh: Edinburgh University Press.

Gray, J. (2005) 'Anti-fandom and the moral text: Television without pity and textual dislike', *American Behavioural Scientist* 48: 840–858.

Gray,J. (2021) Dislike Minded: Media, Audiences and the Dynamics of Taste New York, New York University Press.

Gray, S. and Harrington, C.L. (2007) 'Introduction: Why still study fans?', in Gray, S. and Harrington, C.L. (eds.) *Fandom Identities and Communities in a Mediated World*. New York: New York University Press, pp. 1–26.

Grossberg, L. (1997) *Bringing it all back home*. Durham, NC, Duke University Press.

Grossberg, L. (2010) Affect's Future: Rediscovering the Virtual in the Actual / Lawrence Grossberg interviewed by Gregory Seigworth and Melissa Gress', in Gregg, M. and Seigworth, G.J. (eds.) *The Affect Theory Reader*. Durham, NC: Duke University Press. pp.309–338.

Guo, T. and Evans, J. (2020) 'Translational and transnational queer fandom in China: The fansubbing of carol', *Feminist Media Studies* 20 (4): 515–529.

Harrington, C.L. and Bielby, D. (1995) *Soap Fans: Pursuing Pleasure and Making Meaning in Everyday Life*. Philadelphia: Temple University Press.

Hemmings, C. (2005) 'Invoking affect', *Cultural Studies* 19 (5): 548–567. https://doi.org/10.1080/09502380500365473

Hill, A. (2005) *Reality TV Factual Entertainment and Television Audiences*. Hoboken, NJ: Taylor and Francis.

Hill, A. (2007) *Restyling Factual TV*. London, Routledge.

Hill Collins, P. (2000) *Black Feminist Thought: Knowledge, Consciousness and the Politics of Empowerment*. New York: Routledge.

Hills, M. (2002) *Fan Cultures*. London: Routledge.

Hills, M. (2007) 'Media academic as media audiences: Aesthetic judgements in media and cultural studies', in Gray, S. and Harrington, C.L. (eds.) *Fandom Identities and Communities in a Mediated World*. New York: New York University Press, pp. 33–47.

Hills, K., Paasonen, S., and Petit, M. (eds.). (2015) Introduction in *Networked Affect*. Cambridge, MA: MIT Press.

Hinck, A. (2019) *Politics for the Love of Fandom: Fan-based Citizenship in a Digital World*. Baton Rouge, LA: Louisiana State University Press.

Hochschild, A. (1983) *The Managed Heart: Commericalization of Human Feeling*. Berkeley, CA: University of California Press.

Hobson, D. (1980) *Crossroads: The Drama of a Soap Opera*. London: Methuen.

Huyssen, A. (1986) 'Mass culture as woman: modernism's other', in Modleski, T. (ed.) *Studies in Entertainment*. Bloomington, IN: University of Indiana Press.

Jenkins, H. (2005) 'Why Fiske still matters', Flow, June 10. Available at: https://www.flowjournal.org/2005/06/why-fiske-still-matters (accessed September 10, 2021).

FEEL **115**

Jenkins, H. (1992) *Textual Poachers Television Fans & Participatory Culture*. London and New York: Routledge.

Jensen, T. (2018) *Parenting the Crisis the Cultural Politics of Parent-blame*. Bristol: Policy Press.

Karppi, T. et al. (2016) 'Affective capitalism: Investments and investigations', *Ephemera* 16 (4):1–13.

Kavka, M, (2008) *Reality Television, Affect and Intimacy*: Reality Matters London, Palgrave. pp.1–19.

Kay, J., Kennedy, M. and Wood, H. (2019) 'Something old, something new: the gender politics of the wedding spectacle', in Kay, J. Kennedy, M. and Wood, H (eds.) *The Wedding Spectacle across Contemporary Media and Culture*. London: Routledge.

Kuo, L., Perez-Garcia, S., Burke, L., Yamasaki, V., and Le, T. (2020) 'Performance, fantasy, or narrative: LGBTQ Asian American identity through Kpop Media and Fandom', *Journal of Homosexuality* 1: 145–168.

Lawler, S. (2000) *Mothering the Self: Mothers, Daughters, Subjects*. London: Routledge.

Lovink, G. (2019) *Sad by Design*. London: Pluto Press.

Leys, R. (2017) *The Ascent of Affect: Genealogy and Critique*. Chicago, IL: University of Chicago Press.

Lunenborg, M. and Maier, T. (2019) 'Analysing affective media practices by use of video analysis', In Kahl, A. (ed.) *Analysing Affective Societies*. London: Routledge.

Mankekar, P. (1999) *Screening Culture: Viewing Politics: An Ethnography of Television, Womanhood, and Nation in Postcolonial India*. Durham, NC: Duke University Press.

Massumi, B. (1993) *Politics of Everyday Fear*. Minneapolis: University of Minnesota Press.

Massumi, B. (2002) *Parables for the Virtual: Movement, Affect, Sensation*. Durham, NC: Duke University Press.

Massumi, B. (2010) '2 The Future Birth of the Affective Fact: The Political Ontology of Threat', in Melissa Gregg and Gregory J. Seigworth (eds.) *The Affect Theory Reader*. New York: Duke University Press, pp. 52–70.

Mattia, B. (2018) 'Rainbow direction and fan-based citizenship performance', *The Future of Fandom*, special 10th anniversary issue Transformative Works and Cultures 28. http://dx.doi.org/10.3983/twc.2018.1414.

McChesney, R.W. (1996) 'Communication for the hell of it: The triviality of U.S. broadcasting history', Journal of Broadcasting and Electronic Media 40: 540–552.

McInroy, L.B., Zapcic, I., and Beer, O.W.J. (2022) 'Online fandom communities as networked counterpublics: LGBTQ youths' perceptions of representation and community climate', *Convergence* (London, England) 28 (3): 629–647.

McRobbie, A. (2008) *The Aftermath of Feminism: Gender, Culture and Social Change* (1st ed.). Culture, Representation and Identity Series. London: SAGE Publications.

Morley, D. (1980) *The Nationwide Audience*. London: BFI.

116 FEEL

Morley, D. (1986) *Family Television: Cultural Power and Domestic Leisure*. London: Comedia Pub. Group (Comedia series, no. 37).

Ngai, S. (2005) *Ugly Feelings*. Cambridge, MA: Harvard University Press.

Ouellette, L. and Hay, J. (2008) *Better Living Through Reality TV: Television and Post-welfare Citizenship*. Oxford: Blackwell Publishing.

Paasonen S. (2021) *Dependant, Distracted, Bored*. Cambridge, MA: MIT Press.

Papacharissi, Z. (2015) 'Affective publics and structures of storytelling: sentiment, events and mediality', *Information, Communication & Society*. https://doi.org/10.1080/1369118X.2015.1109697

Papacharizzi, Z. (2014) *Affective Publics: Sentiment, Technology, Politics*. Oxford: Oxford University Press.

Penley, C. (1992) 'Feminism, psychoanalysis, and the study of popular culture', in Lawrence Grossberg, Cary Nelson and Paula Treichler (eds.) *Cultural Studies*. New York & London: Routledge. pp. 479–500.

Probyn, E. (2005) *Blush: Faces of Shame*. Minneapolis, MN: University of Minnesota Press.

Punathambekar, A. (2007) 'Between Rowdies and Rasika: Rethinking fan activity in Indian Film Culture', in Gray, J., et al. (eds.) *Fandom: Identities and Communities in a Mediated Era*. New York: New York University Press.

Sandvoss, C. (2012) 'Enthusiasm, trust and its erosion in mediated politics: On fans of Obama and the liberal democrats', *European Journal of Communication* 27 (1): 68–81. https://doi.org/10.1177/0267323111435296

Seigworth, G. (2018) 'Foreward', in Sampson, T, Maddisson, S and Ellis, D (eds.) *Affect and Social Media*. Rowman and Littlefield. pp. xi–xiii.

Seiter, E. (1990) 'Making distinctions in TV audience research: Case study of a troubling interview', *Cultural Studies* 4: 61–84. https://doi.org/10.1080/09502389000490051

Sender, K. (2012) *The Makeover: Reality Television and Reflexive Audiences*. Critical Cultural Communication Series. New York: New York University Press.

Skeggs, B. (2004) 'Exchange, Value and Affect: Bourdieu and 'the self'' in Adkins, L. and Skeggs, B. (eds.) *Feminism After Bourdieu*. Oxford: Blackwell. pp.75–95.

Skeggs, B. and Wood, H. (2008) 'Spectacular morality: Reality television, individu-alisation and the re-making of the working class', in Hesmondhalgh, D and Toynbee, J. (eds.) *The Media and Social Theory*. London: Routledge. pp.177–193.

Skeggs, B., Thumim, N. and Wood, H. (2008) '"Oh goodness, I am watching Reality TV": How methods make class in multi-method audience research', *European Journal of Cultural Studies* 11 (1): 5–24.

Skeggs, B. and Wood, H. (2012) *Reacting to Reality Television: Audience, performance and value*. London and New York: Routledge.

Spivak, G. C. (1993) 'Woman in difference', in Spivak, G.C. (ed.) *Outside in the Teaching Machine*. New York: Routledge, pp. 77/95.

Stacey, J. (2004) *Star Gazing: Hollywood Cineman and Female Spectatorship*. London and New York: Routledge.

Stanfill, M. (2019). *Exploiting Fandom: How the Media Industry Seeks to Manipulate Fans*. Iowa, University of Iowa Press

Striphas, T. (2015) 'Algorithmic culture', *European Journal of Cultural Studies* 18 (4–5): 395–412.

Thornton, S. (1995) *Club Cultures: Music, Media and Subcultural Capital*. Cambridge: Polity Press.

Thrift, N. (2007) *Non-representation Theory: Space, Politics, Affect*. London: Routledge.

Tyler, I. (2008) 'Chav Mum Chav Scum', *Feminist Media Studies* 8 (1): 17–34.

Wahl-Jorgensen, K. (2019) *Emotions, Media and Politics*. London: Polity.

Wetherell, M. (2012) *Affect and Emotion: A New Social Science Understanding*. London: Sage.

Weber, B. (2009) *Makeover TV: Selfhood, Citizenship, and Celebrity*. Durham NC: Duke University Press.

White, M. (1992) *Tele-advising: Therapeutic Discourse in American Television*. Chapel Hill, NC: University of North Carolina Press.

Williams, R. (1961) *The Long Revolution*. New York, Chichester, West Sussex: Columbia University Press.

Williams, R. (1977) *Marxism and Culture*. Oxford: Oxford University Press.

Wood, H. (2018) 'The Magaluf Girl: A public sex scandal and the digital class relations of social contagion', *Feminist Media Studies* 8 (4): 626–642.

Yoon, T.-J., Jin, D.Y., Fung, A.Y.H., Hong, S.-K., Huang, L., Jung, H., Kang, B., Kim, J.O., and Lee, E. (2017) *The Korean Wave: Evolution, Fandom, and Transnationality*. Blue Ridge Summit, PA: Lexington Books.

5

WORK

SCENARIO: THE CREATOR UNION

August of 2020 saw the launch of 'The Creator Union' in the UK as an attempt to provide a collective voice for content creators (which include YouTubers, Bloggers, TikTokers, Instagrammars, podcasters, Twitchers) anyone who creates digital content and is attempting to monetise their output in the increasingly lucrative arena of influencer marketing. The value of influencer marketing in the UK is estimated to reach £17.4bn in 2024.[1] The development of a trade union is related to the rapid rise in this new employment arena without regulatory oversight, or any standardisation of contractual agreements between influencers and brands. According to co-founder Nicola Orcran, '... with long, irregular hours, irregularity of pay and pay disparity, no pensions, no holiday pay – this is the time to negotiate for better terms for ourselves for the work that we do'.[2] Such concerns over this relatively chaotically-emerging arena has also led to a UK Parliamentary Inquiry in 2021[3] which unearthed evidence about exploitative practices in contractual arrangements, problems with a lack of diversity and inclusivity, and increasing mental health problems related to nature of the exposure of personal lives for content, and the growth of

DOI: 10.4324/9781003414575-6

online hate and trolling. The inquiry made a number of suggestions: for instance support for safer working environments especially for children, the standardisation of rates, and more powers to Ofcom (the UK communications regulator) to hold platforms to account.

I draw on this example here for how it is emblematic of the ways in which contemporary questions of audiences as 'users' now must navigate the very explicit arena of work and employment. Influencers can emerge from the ranks of 'ordinary' people, gaining democratised access to content creation via platforms by building their own 'tribe' of followers based on para-social relationships and trust. This is part of the digital environment where distinctions once central to audience studies collapse – most notably between performer and audience and between producer and consumer (as we discussed in Chapter 1). BBC Newsround's survey of 3,000 children aged 8 to 12 in the UK, United States and China found that children are three times more likely to want to be a YouTuber than an Astronaut.[4] This demonstrates the ways in which the participatory platform environment is creating new career pathways that are open to new forms of exploitation. Whilst there are some mechanisms by which profitable platforms remunerate their successful users, the UK inquiry heard that ByteDance (owners of TikTok) made \$58billion in profits in 2021 whilst only paying out \$200million to the creators who generate its content[5]. A 'user' monetising their content here becomes a worker, but there is a longer history to the entwining of audiences with the structures of capital accumulation and work, which this chapter will explore.

QUESTION: DO AUDIENCES WORK?

It may seem odd to consider that what we are doing as members of an audience is 'work'. Watching TV, theatre, film and reading newspapers, magazines, etc. were more likely to be characterised as belonging to our 'non-work' time, our 'free' time or our leisure time. We usually consider what we do as part of an audience as connected to pleasure, or possibly getting information, which are not traditionally thought of as analogous to work. Work under industrial capitalism has mostly been characterised as tiresome upon the body and tedious for the mind. Nevertheless, as we have seen in this book, increasingly we are participating in various

120 WORK

aspects of the media and generating our own content, which for the relatively few successful social media influencers or YouTube sensations can end up sustaining a lucrative career. The rise of social media entertainment involves content delivered by global platforms such as YouTube, Facebook, Instagram, Snapchat, Twitch and TikTok that Cunningham and Craig (2019: 71) describe as

> an emerging proto-industry based on previously amateur creators professionalising and engaging in content innovation and media entrepreneurship across multiple social media platforms to aggregate global fan communities and incubate their own media brands.

These kind of media careers are offering various opportunities whereby the boundaries between work and leisure have become in increasingly blurred, mirroring the broader more precarious and flexible nature of work in contemporary advanced capitalist societies and often been supported by an ideological ethos towards work known as 'doing what you love' (Ross, 2009).

In this chapter, I want to set out the older arguments about audience activity as work that have started out in the political economy tradition. I then want to bring to bear ideas about the economic and ideological shifts in what constitutes work under contemporary capitalism. This involves a broader orientation towards thinking of aspects of personal lives *as* work that are visible in popular media such as models of self-branding. From here, I want to draw out the many ways in which various aspects of audience activity from fan engagements to influencer activity have been considered as 'labour' in which there has been a revival of arguments from the Frankfurt School that we discussed briefly in Chapter 2. I want to conclude with a discussion of what it might mean for audience analysis to adopt the lens of labour and work that assumes a total absorption of activity into forms of capital, and make some suggestions about its impact upon traditional audience analysis of meaning-making and culture.

AUDIENCE COMMODITY

Given the rise of the influencer industry and the prevalence of creative fan content online, it might seem surprising that being part of a television audience (especially if you ever believed in the term 'couch potato') has also been thought about under the terms of 'work'. The Frankfurt School (which we discussed briefly in Chapter 2) via Max Horkeimer and Theodor Adorno in 1947 offered a critique of the culture industries as providing distraction from our working conditions. This in turn enables and supports the capitalist system itself – not just by securing consent for its ideas – but also by drawing the workers time away from other perhaps more revolutionary and resistive practices, thereby maintaining the status quo. If you recall from Chapter 3, Marxist analysts have been concerned with the power of ideologies of the media securing consent for a capitalist system. This dominated some of the work which was concerned with the 'messages' of the media as a manufacturer of ideas which support its own (capitalist) logics and how these might then be passed on to audiences. This relies on an economistic model in which the economy becomes entirely responsible for ideology and whilst I am simplifying here for brevity, in media studies this belongs to the Political Economy tradition. Cultural Studies, influenced by scholars such as Raymond Williams, felt this position too 'reductionist', presuming too simplified and direct relationship with the economy and ignoring the role of culture and lived experience in history.

Missing from debates about ideology and about the consideration of the 'political economy' of the mass media was an understanding of the audience as also a commodity under monopoly capitalism. Dallas Smythe (1977) is credited for opening-up this position when he argued that mass media systems that rely on advertising to create revenue, deliver audiences, and audience-demographics, to advertisers that continues the demand upon production. One of the most radical suggestions was that our spare time is not our 'free' time at all but as long as we are part of an audience situated in front of advertisements then our free time, much like our waged work time, has been 'sold'. However, we have not been in control of selling this time, as is perhaps the case with waged labour, rather the mass media corporations have sold our time to advertisers the moment we take our place as part of an audience.

This model relies on the Marxist distinction between different forms of labour. There is productive labour, which is our productivity through the waged relation which goes into the making of a product and from

122 WORK

which we have become increasingly alienated under capitalism; and our 'capacity to labour' which is the mental and physical capacities of a human-being that we bring to the production and the generation of use value. Marketing and advertising therefore, according to Smythe (1977) involve us in activities of 'free labour' because '["our"] time which is sold to advertisers (a) perform essential marketing functions for the producers of consumers' goods, and (b) work at the production and reproduction of labour power' (1977: 3).

Perhaps one of the very clever tricks of the system is that being part of an audience does not 'feel' like work at all. It does not necessarily make us physically tired or weary, but for Smythe it does involve us in specific tasks that are useful to capitalism. We learn which particular brands to buy and spend our income accordingly. In doing so we help to create demand for advertised goods and therefore 'whilst doing this audiences are simultaneously reproducing their own labour power' (1977: 6). Dallas Smythe's work was developed by Jhally and Livant (1986) to further establish the relationship between television audiences and work. However, they made an important distinction – for them the labour provided by the audience was not directly 'for' the advertising industry, but mostly for the television companies and networks. For them the viewing audience receive payment through 'free' programming for which they supply 'surplus attention' that is sold on to the advertisers by the media companies. Eileen Meehan (2013) also points out the need for a feminist re-evaluation of the political economy of the 'audience commodity' pointing out how television rating industries over-valued the male audience, whilst dismissing the gendered feminised daytime audience, just as it dismissed the value of their labour in the home. This is a point we should bear in mind when we consider the debates about user-generated-content and its relationship to the feminised labour of unpaid social reproduction later in this chapter.

AUDIENCES AS PERFORMERS

One of the biggest changes delivered by new platforms has been the dissolution of boundaries between audiences and performers that both muddies, and at the same time extends, this older model about delivering audiences directly to advertisers. This has a longer

WORK 123

history than the evolution of YouTube, as the press, radio and television have long traditions of including their audiences *in* the media, examples such as 'letters to the editor', radio phone-ins and of course the development of the vox-pop, quiz shows, observational documentary, talks shows and reality television (see Griffen-Foley, 2004). These trends have occurred prior to the arrival of social media, but also in many ways have laid the ground for the development of these newer spaces of self-performance – of audiences-becoming-performers – across the media (Wood, 2017). In the talk show, the audience is invited onto the stage to facilitate a connection between the audience at home and the audience in the studio as part of television's strategies for achieving intimacy through its 'para-social address' and inviting us to 'feel' part of the show as it unfolds (Wood, 2009). On reality television audiences are invited to think of ourselves as the potential 'stars' of the show. In many ways, the audience at home are the new workforce in a television environment that has struggled in competing with the internet for advertising revenue. Therefore, the television industry has turned to the audience into its latest resource or 'raw material' and one that it does not have to pay reality participants in the same way that it has to pay actors or celebrities (Raphael, 2009).

Whilst this suggests a literal turning to the audience as 'workers' or 'commodities' in the service of production, it is accompanied with an ideological drive in which reality television orients our association to self-performance as work, that has arguably prepared the ground for the influencer industry described above. Mark Andrejevic (2003) in *Reality TV: The work of being watched,* pointed to the relationship between the rise of reality television and our accommodation of surveillance technology. He suggests that shows like *Big Brother* and *The Real World* using CCTV technology helped audiences become accustomed to the idea of 'being watched' – a situation that has arisen out of the development of techniques in the modern capitalist workplace where the worker is surveilled to assure their productivity. Reality TV turns 'being watched' into a commodity for television which is part of an increasingly sophisticated landscape through which all our activities are monitored and tracked in processes of mass-customisation to better enable the identification of further needs and serve new and evolving markets.

124 WORK

This landscape is abetted by broad social and cultural shifts as Charles Taylor (1989, 1991) and Marilyn Strathern (1992) identify, where traditional structures of validation such as religion and the state have receded in modern societies, and so we must perform our self-worth to others in processes of 'compulsory individuality'. Anthony Giddens (1991) similarly refers to the 'reflexive project of the self' where we must constantly evaluate ourselves to suit the demands of the market economy. This involves ensuring that we have the right look, the right mind-set, the right ambition, the right family, the friendship networks, the right commodities and so on, in order to succeed in an ultra-competitive neoliberal economic environment. A plethora of lifestyle media forms offer us some of the resources to do this self-work and indeed some argue give us lessons in exactly *how* to perform self-work positioning audiences as potential 'workers' ready for neoliberal capitalism. Consider the rise of 'spectacular subjectivity' in first-person television which increasingly includes tenets and lessons in self-evaluation and self-reflection (Dovey, 2000). From the 1990s talk-show, to lifestyle make-over television, to more contemporary forms of reality television, the in-built potential of the 'TV format' continually opens out our ways of life to public scrutiny (Weber, 2009; Skeggs and Wood, 2012). In these ways frames of measurement and self-evaluation, developed under longer histories of capital-relations, have been extended and promoted (Skeggs and Wood, 2012). Ouellette and Hay (2008) insist that reality television offers audiences lessons in taking care of oneself in an environment where welfare support is being eroded and where neoliberal frames of governance privilege ideologies of self-reliability and self-governance:

> It prepares the worker to take on burdens of insecurity and disposability in the name of his or her own freedom, and provides them with the tenuous resources for navigating the impossibility of this task.
>
> (2008: 101)

Annette Hill's (2005) extensive empirical work on reality TV audiences, amongst other insights, demonstrates the way in which some audiences take on board and appropriate those lessons.

WORK 125

FREE LABOUR

Reality television's blurring of the roles of audience and performer corresponds with the evolving space of social media to further complicate the arrangements of audiencing and performing. In the context of participatory culture, Smythe's (1977) thinking on the audience as commodity as involving labour has become more even more central to theorising the nature of the audience in the digital landscape. As our digital imprints are captured and returned as information, even our likes and dislikes enable algorithms to send us relevant advertising and suggestions for our next views or next set of purchases. Almost everything we do online can be used in the service of marketing and in the accumulation of profit – think of the popular phrase: 'If you're not paying for it; you are the product'.[6] Given the participatory environment described in Chapter 1, the revival of accounting for this by using models of labour and exploitation taken from Marx, has provided a welcome relief from some of the more optimistic ideals about the internet's emancipatory potential.

Titziana Terranova (2000) suggests that, 'Free labor is the moment where this knowledgeable consumption of culture is translated into productive activities that are pleasurably embraced and at the same time often shamelessly exploited' (Terranova, 2000: 37). This explains the transition from how we 'feel' about work that we started out with, into monikers like 'do what you love', and you can see how this sits with arguments about 'lovebor' (Stanfill, 2019) in the discussion on fandom that we touched upon Chapter 4 and to which we will return. This relies on detaching the link between labour and employment (a waged contractual agreement) and suggests that the forms of labour that suit the digital economy best are those that rely on the production of information and culture and 'affective' outcomes, rather than the material commodities of the industrial era.

Terranova relies on the theories of the Autonomist Marxists (notably Mauricio Lazzarato, Michael Hardt, Maurizio Lazzarato, Antonio Negri and Paolo Virno in the early 1990s) who refer to this as 'immaterial labour' as 'the labour that produces the information and cultural content of the commodity' (Lazzarato, 1996: 133). Labour that creates value through emotion, affect, culture, style in a combination of cultural/technical/affective production (advertising, marketing, branding, media) constitutes the digital economy. The autonomist Marxists have come under criticism for being overly optimistic about the collective potential of what they term the 'social factory' as well as for ignoring gender relations and feminist intellectual thought about the how less tangible gendered (caring) labour goes unpaid despite its service to the capitalist economy (Jarrett, 2008, 2014, 2016).

This position though is largely accepted as useful to the analysis of user-generated content on social media as 'free labour' that generates income for large platform corporations (Jarrett, 2022). Here, the use of surveillance capabilities of digital capture enable our energies on social media to be harnessed for the profit of others' and user-generated content becomes 'labour' that can be exploited (see Fuchs, 2011a, 2011b; Jarrett, 2022). Consider the size of the profit generated by ByteDance relative to its payments to TikTok content creators that we opened with in this chapter. In this sense, when we take part in social media, we are also engaging in the labour and production of ourselves and our lives as commodities to be bought and sold.

FAN LABOUR

As discussed in the last chapter, an analysis of the ways user-generated content gets raided for commercial advantage by the mainstream media, raises numerous questions about the exploitation of fandom's 'gift-economy' (see also, Baym and Burnett, 2009; Scott, 2015; Proctor, 2021). Abigail De Kosnik (2016) discusses the volunteer labour of fan communities and their online archiving activities, whilst critics have outlined the deliberate incorporation of fan practices into marketing and profit-making strategies for media companies. Mark Andrejevic (2008) discussed the way in which online fan message boards provide value-enhancing labour for television producers. Joyce Goggin (2018) discusses the way in which Lego even 'farmed' the free fan production of 'brick movies' in order to make the LEGO movie, without much resistance. This is largely due to the affective ties generated by the brand amassing soaring profits for Lego. Mel Stanfill (2019) further details the extensive way in which fan-industry relations have developed through the incorporation and domestication of fan exploitation through which fan activities easily become incorporated into media industry logics and marketing.

Here emotional investments and affective states contribute to the production of 'affective labour' that only adds surplus value to the brand in ways which exploit the emotional investments that we discussed in Chapter 4. For instance, Anselmo's (2018) analysis of Tumblr blogs dedicated to queer readings of the BBC television series *Sherlock* discusses the unremunerated queer labour of 'utopian, heuristic, and care work' enabled by digital interactivity and storytelling. If this is the natural evolutionary home of the active-audience tradition, it is with a renewed caution and scepticism of the ways in which 'activity' can be so readily exploited by capital. Perhaps one of the major achievements of this turn to audience labour is that it counters some of the criticism of the 'over-celebratory' ideas of the resistive potential of active-audience studies, fan studies and participatory culture.

SELF-BRANDING

Even outside of the free labour provided by fans, the ubiquity of focussed self-management encouraged by many popular media forms twinned to the needs of the market has paved the way for the potentially total colonisation of our lived experiences. Attributes of our personal lives are ripe for capital accumulation in a process now commonly discussed as 'self-branding'. It exists as part of a context of that Wernick (1991) refers to as 'promotionalism': where according to David Harvey, 'the acquisition of an image… becomes a singularly important element of the presentation of the self in labour markets' (Harvey, 1990: 288, cited in Hearn, 2008). For Alison Hearn (2008) this as a distinct form of labour under post-Fordist capitalism where:

> Self-branding involves the construction of a meta-narrative and meta-image of self through the construction of cultural meanings and images drawn from the narratives and visual codes of the mainstream cultural industries.
>
> (2008: 195)

Sarah Banet-Weiser (2012: 13) in her work on brand culture suggests an increasing blurring between any sense of an 'authentic self' and a 'commodity self' – a once seemingly untenable position that is now

128 WORK

both 'accepted and tolerated'. Consider the ways in which we are encouraged to promote details of ourselves in the social media landscape and the ways in which 'your story', your likes, your locations, the places you visit, your connections and so on, are all visible (even if you have altered your privacy settings), to the platform and service provider. According to Eran Fisher, 'When one first joins Facebook as a member, this audience member has no content to consume; audiencing begins when one connects with other audience members, becoming in fact *their* audience.' (2015: 63). In these conditions, audiencing is also marketing in the digital landscape.

Audience labour theory has therefore had to keep up with these developments extending consideration of how audience time is bought (in keeping with Marxist theories of labour), and has been concerned with the way audiences now work to 'produce' content and data. Here data is the newest 'raw material' in Marxist terms that is put to use in the service of capital accumulation (Fuchs, 2011b). Facebook's Sponsored Stories are a case in point: everyday location check-ins are sponsored by a commercial enterprise and elevated on the platform to reach larger audiences. This is monetising our everyday experiences and fine-targeting commercial products to our own social groups. Furthermore, companies do not have to do much for this service, since *we* do that for them. Users literally do the marketing, build their own networks and even maintain the platform content through constant curation, updating and uploading life events. Fisher (2015: 65) refers to this as 'reality advertising' where the audience *is* the media.

This 'attention economy' of the digital landscape, founded upon more entrepreneurial labour models, encourages the constant leveraging of advantage through an emphasis upon individual promotion. The notion of 'you' media, from YouTube to social networking to TikTok means that there are developing styles of online performance whereby we perform and audience for our networks with the aim of building bigger audiences or numbers of followers. In Theresa Senft's (2008) book on 'Camgirls' she coins the term 'micro-celebrity' to capture the developing apparatus for the girls in her study to 'amp up' their popularity on-line. In this way rather than traditional celebrity referencing something that one 'is' as a result of fame achieved through another means, micro-celebrity through vlogging, etc. becomes something that one 'does' in order to achieve fame. This 'micro-celebrity'

WORK **129**

relies on models of audiencing through 'para-social interaction' and creating an 'intimacy at a distance' (Horton and Wohl, 1956) which is established in older media and we have discussed as an anchor to contemporary models of influencer culture in Chapter 2. Research on the work of influencing stresses how much hard work goes into the building of a brand (Abidin, 2016; Duffy, 2017). First you build the brand, then you build the audience and then you might get economic compensation, in the reverse of most existing previous labour models (Marwick, 2013). Becoming celebrity is the very process, the work, and the end game.

INFLUENCER STUDIES

This brings us to where we began this chapter, with the growing field of 'influencer studies' which analyses how 'ordinary' users now gain access to generate commercial advantages and even brand sponsorship deals which has spurned the most numerous attention to forms of 'digital labour'. Many of the analyses of this phenomena refer to the energy espoused in producing content for free in order to generate some deferred return down the line, which draws on models well-established in the creative industries using platforms to freely advertise their creative work. For instance, Brooke Erin Duffy (2016) refers to the 'aspirational labour' of fashion and beauty vloggers which draws on highly gendered labour forms. Duffy's (2017) work reveals some of the pain and hard work behind scenes of the apparent glamourous lifestyle of vloggers. For her research respondents, the 'incessant schedule of planning, styling, writing, and networking was taxing' (2017: 186) whilst few attain success. Vlogging also requires a hyper-vigilance about one's online persona accompanied by an ongoing and perpetual state of 'always on' entrepreneurialism.

The generation of these numerous forms of 'immaterial labour' in the production and creation of online communities is extended in the image-led platform of Instagram whereby promotional culture and social networking conflate. Crystal Abidin (2015) again using concepts drawn from 'para-social interaction' (Horton and Wohl, 1956) discusses the 'intimacy labour' involved in securing and accumulating followers, sharing personal disclosures and maintaining relationships. Abidin describes the numerous aspects of maintaining self-promotion under the umbrella term, 'visibility labour' which she describes as, 'the work individuals do when they self-posture and curate their self-presentations so as to be noticeable and positively prominent among prospective employers (Neff et al., 2005), clients (Duffy, 2016), the press (Wissinger, 2015)' (2016: online). Followers then also become involved in the 'tacit labour' of becoming involved in the 're-grams' of advertorials, reposting with hashtags etc. further offering up free labour in the building of relationships for the brand (Abidin, 2016). Literature on 'viral' advertising in marketing attends to the many and complex ways in which the participatory framework of online media directly incorporates the audience into the game.

Cunningham and Craig's (2019) discussion of what they called the 'social media entertainment industries' describes the way in which YouTubers engage in the work of 'being really real' which they call 'authenticity labour' following Banet-Weiser's attention to the way in which 'being real' is potently at stake in commercial culture. They consider the particularly skilled discursive modes of address that belongs to the online environment of social media entertainment through which community building (much like in early broadcasting) is the main goal. Banet-Weiser (2021) alludes to the competitive way in which this evolves on Instagram for largely female influencers who must do the 'labour of authenticity' as part of maintaining their visibility, showing also their vulnerabilities, in a highly competitive and increasingly professionalised environment, which is structurally uneven and unequal – a point to which we will return.

IS IT EXPLOITATION?

The conversations about 'audience labour' ran into difficult territory because the total appropriation of our attributes into the service of capital, then extends to the idea that *everything* we do is labour since it is mediated, and *everything* is exploitable in that it is turned into some form of data: Thus *everything* is work. There is a problem here if we treat all differing forms of labour as the same: paid, unpaid, free, immaterial and emotional. The labour used to create new digital technologies in sweatshops, usually in the global south, is of course not the same as the labour offered by a Star Trek fan in the reproduction of their favourite narratives in vlogs.

WORK **131**

For David Hesmondhalgh (2010) the issue is that in many of the debates about 'free labour' have been too easily coupled up to ideas of 'exploitation' which perhaps makes light of more serious forms of exploitation and injustice. Hesmondhalgh (2010) asks us to use the term more precisely, drawing upon the sociologist Erik Olin Wright (1997) who spells out that there are three ways in which exploitation exists in the Marxist sense which:

- First, exploitation occurs when the material welfare of one class is causally dependent upon the material deprivation of another. The capitalist class in modern societies could not exist without the deprivations of the working classes.
- Second, that causal dependence depends in turn on the exclusion of workers from key productive resources, especially property.
- Third, the mechanism through which both these features (causal dependence and exclusion) operate is appropriation of the labour of the exploited. The first two alone would just represent oppression; for exploitation (in the Marxian sense) to take place, the third condition must be present.

it 'Appropriation is not the same thing as exploitation; the first two features, causal dependence and exclusion, must also be present as well as appropriation.' (Hesmondhalgh, 2010: 274) What this begins to open out is that given there is some autonomy in the practices of 'free labour' just because the effects are appropriated and turned into surplus value, it does not mean that is necessarily suggests exploitation in the Marxist sense.

Goran Bolin (2012) argues that at the centre of the free labour debates is a misunderstanding around ideas about the collapse of the distinction between production and consumption. He suggests that all modes of production have always required some level of consumption (the tools for the job for instance) and all consumption has always involved some level of production (the production of symbolic ideas of self through commodities). '"Production", said Marx (1939/1993, p. 91), "is also immediately consumption, consumption is also immediately production"' (Cited in Bolin, 2012) but that does not necessarily mean that the boundaries are collapsed – rather that they operate in distinct fields (borrowing from Bourdieu) and attest

132 WORK

to two separate circuits. The 'work' that audiences do in the 'active audiences' paradigm that involves interpretative work that serves to support identity-building or 'identity-work' is entirely separate to the 'work' that machine-algorithms do in the aggregation of our data for profit. This for Bolin, citing Eileen Meehan points to the weak-spot in the original 'audience labour' theory which misrecognised the work of statisticians for the work of audiences – and now in the era of social media *that* work is adopted by the computer driven algorithm rather than the audience.

This does not mean that the practices of platforms are not at all exploitative, but rather that they are not exploitative in *exactly* the same way. As Bev Skeggs and Simon Yuill (2019) argue there are clearly forms of exploitation at work, but they are not the same as the exploitation of time and labour through energy, as in previous capitalist societies. They discuss the inequities drawn through Facebook's use of data as 'property' describing how Facebook capitalise on one person's networks (the middle-class enterprising subject) as the perfect digital subject for them to aggregate their data and target advertising accordingly. However, other users who are less invested in the platform and who may be careful of exposing their personal data for reasons (such as surveillance from the Department for Work and Pensions in the UK) are less targeted and tracked and less aggregated, although their data is stored for such a time as when it becomes useful. Facebook decides who has value and who has not by means of the harvesting of their personal data as their own property through IP. When we sign up to Facebook we sign over all of our data and we enable them to track our internet browser history beyond our Facebook interactions.

> What advertisers buy is not so much the time of our attention, nor the labour of our looking [...], but rather the timeliness of a momentary correlation between attributes and desires (or desperations) through which the possibility of response (click-throughs being the most profitable adverts) may be ever more finely attuned. It is in those moments of attuned disaggregation that money is made.
>
> (Skeggs and Yuill, 2019: 94)

In this sense social media 'data-banking' becomes like that of land-banking of property developers 'who buy up empty buildings and

WORK 133

'waste ground alike to monopolise their value when the market turns away' (Skeggs and Yuill, 2019: 94). These are new mechanisms for extracting value from subjects which work to extend existing inequalities as we have also discussed in Chapter 1 in terms of the ways in which algorithms and automation can perpetuate injustice.

A FEMINISED SPHERE AND INFLUENCER INEQUALITIES

Kylie Jarrett's (2014, 2016, 2021) feminist analysis insists that user-generated-content is labour (even if it is not always exploited) because it operates very much like the undervalued sphere of social reproduction (the work that women often do) in the service of capitalism. She argues that it is as though, 'immaterial labour was invented the moment it came out of the kitchen and onto the internet' (2014: 15). Feminist theorists have long argued that we need to consider the broader spheres of home, care and the *social* in the reproduction of the worker to the value of capitalism (Fraser, Dalla Costa and James, 1972; Federici, 2004; Davis, 2019). Jarrett argues that in digital labour we need to continue to understand these broader social relations which create the conditions for work: 'This takes us beyond moments of commodity production where labour is producing goods that are sold in the marketplace to other places where other activity produces self, subjectivities and bodies that sustain and support capital' (2022: 30).

Here user-generated-content is the very essence of digital capitalism and various studies offer a discussion of the unseen work and time that goes into influencer careers: the scouting for locations, the setting up, the planning and the increasing professionalisation and use of equipment in developing in a short piece of content for YouTube or TikTok (Pham, 2015; Cunningham and Craig, 2019; Bucher and Shannon, 2020). In digital labour across all sectors, there is persistent and chronic under-compensation for time and an acceptance of precarious working conditions which is often attached to subjective and psychic associations related to entrepreneurialism and an insistence of an self-development and self-evaluation which supports a lack formalised collective networks for workers (Jarrett, 2022).

Whilst Kylie Jarrett's (2022) *Digital Labour* discusses the more complex alignments and distinctions between user-generated-content and other forms of platform labour, here I want to consider what this might mean for the development of audience studies. In many ways we can see the attention on influencers, an extremely feminised sphere of the digital economy, as reminiscent of the 1980s work on soap opera which sought to validate and open up women's attachments and 'emotional labour' to academic scrutiny and understand its relationship to broader social relations. A study like Crystal Abidin's essay on selfies 'Aren't These Just Young, Rich Women Doing Vain Things Online?': Influencer Selfies as Subversive Frivolity'. Seems to offer just such a re-appraisal of potential of the dismissed feminised sphere and acknowledges agentive practices at work in the labours of visibility.

Whilst it is clear that this is indeed part of the work, its appraisal must also be accompanied by social critique, after all we are concerned with the role of media and audiences in the production and reproduction of the social order. For Jarrett, 'the relationship between affective labor and capitalism is not always direct […] In a multiphase process of commodification, what is exploitative at one moment of the circuit may not be so at another' (2014: 25). The complexity of the sets of arrangements, however, should not deter us from also considering the relationships between particular cases and instances and their role in the reproduction of inequalities. Marwick's (2013) analysis of the tech scene suggests that self-branding works best for those who can most easily draw on the resources necessary to improve their status – who she calls the 'digital elite' who entrench existing axes of power. There is the acknowledgement that entry into digital labour practices is not even – for instance, Safiya Noble's (2018) account of racist algorithms of oppression which we discuss Chapter 6. Sophie Bishop (2018) has also pointed to the way in which algorithmic hierarchies privilege middle-class influencers on YouTube and that items such as closed captioning disadvantages regional accents. Those that are mostly likely to succeed in the influencer industry are white middle-class cis gendered women who conform to euro-centric beauty ideals (Banet-Weiser, 2021). Agentive practices in participatory cultures are not therefore upending longer histories of inequality.

Early feminist work on the role of the mass media was concerned with the 'symbolic annihilation' (Tuchman, 1978) of women whereby questions of the representation of women, and their absence from particular narratives and accounts of public life were important. These struggles still continue, but for audience studies, the 'struggle' that we need now also to attend to is not just the struggle over meaning and ideology and the symbolic (Chapter 3) but a struggle over symbolic annihilation through which algorithmic sets of calculation hierarchise the symbolic realm. Bolin's (2012) argument that, 'the work that serves to support identity-building or "identity-work" is entirely separate to the 'work' that machine-algorithms do in the aggregation of our data for profit,' does not quite acknowledge the interdependency of one with the other. It also does not help enable a conversation about the ideological consent for the acceptance of neoliberal frameworks of existence such as in the era of self-branding, which rely on both ideologies of calculation and competition *as well as* their technical implementation in digital networks. This requires a close analysis of culture and the conjunctural moment in order to weave the intricate seams of these aspects together which we will go on to discuss in the next chapter.

CONCLUSION

In answering the question *'Do audiences work*?' I have accounted for the ways in which audience attachments and engagements are imbricated in the work of capitalist societies. These involve arguments about audiencing as labour, and the audience's role in the accumulation of profits beyond their purchasing power as consumers. I began with an account largely derived from the position of the political economy thesis that considered the audience as a commodity in the mass media era. We moved on to discuss how in participatory media these questions have resurfaced, largely as user-generated-content offers up 'free labour' for capital. We considered the way in which the groundwork for considering ourselves as marketable entities, such that 'life is a pitch' (Gill, 2011) have been ideologically established by the media narratives and incorporated and 'lived' in our online worlds. Some of those taking up the call to live 'life as work' and simultaneously 'work as life' are now beginning to see the deeply precarious and difficult working conditions that such forms beget, such that there is the need for a 'Creators Union', the scenario with which we opened this chapter.

The challenge for audience studies when distinctions collapse between audience and performer and performer as audience, as is now

136 WORK

the case, is whether we even hold on to our founding questions of meaning in order to understand the contemporary conjuncture? We may drop the attachment to 'audiences' altogether in the descriptions of 'user' activities which detail strategies of optimisation as they navigate platform affordances. But in the next chapter, I want to go on to argue that to hold onto a Cultural Studies' notion of 'audience' is to also hold onto a particular way of seeing the ongoing significance of the cultural realm to the digital environment. This requires continuing the project of Cultural Studies that sees culture as productive and applying it *across* the digital circuit in which the realm of culture and its relationship to social practices represents as much as a maelstrom as it ever did, as I argued in Chapter 1.

NOTES

1 https://news.sky.com/story/why-online-influencers-and-creatives-need-a-union-12036302 (accessed May 26, 2023).
2 https://news.sky.com/story/why-online-influencers-and-creatives-need-a-union-12036302
3 https://publications.parliament.uk/pa/cm5802/cmselect/cmcumeds/258/report.html (accessed May 27, 2023).
4 21 BBC, 'YouTuber or astronaut: Which job would you rather have?' https://www.bbc.co.uk/newsround/49126668 (accessed May 26, 2023).
5 'Influencer Culture: Lights Camera Action' Report of the 12th session of the Parliamentary Inquiry into influencer culture. https://publications.parliament.uk/pa/cm5802/cmselect/cmcumeds/258/report.html (date accessed May 27 2023)
6 "if you're not paying for the product, you are the product" is often attributed to internet entrepreneur and venture capitalist Marc Andreessen. It is believed that he first used this phrase in a blog post in 2010, in which he discussed the business models of various internet companies.

REFERENCES

Abidin, C. (2015) 'Communicative intimacies: Influencers and perceived interconnectedness', *Ada: A Journal of Gender, New Media, & Technology* 8. Available at: https://scholarsbank.uoregon.edu/xmlui/handle/1794/26365
Abidin, C. (2016) 'Visibility labour: Engaging with Influencers' fashion brands and #OOTD advertorial campaigns on Instagram', *Media International Australia* 161 (1): 86–100.
Andrejevic, M. (2003) *Reality TV: The Work of Being Watched*. Critical Media Studies. Lanham, MD: Rowman & Littlefield Publishers.

WORK **137**

Andrejevic, M. (2008) 'Watching television without pity: The productivity of online fans', *Television & New Media* 9 (1): 24–46.

Anselmo, D. W. (2018) 'Gender and queer fan labor on Tumblr', *Feminist Media Histories* 4 (1): 84–114.

Banet-Weiser, S. (2012) *AuthenticTM: The Politics of Ambivalence in a Brand Culture*. New York: New York University Press.

Banet-Weiser, S. (2021) 'Gender, social media, and the labor of authenticity', *American Quarterly* 73 (1): 141–144.

Baym, N.K. and Burnett, R. (2009) 'Amateur experts', *International Journal of Cultural Studies* 12 (5): 433–449.

Bishop, S. (2018). Anxiety, panic and self-optimization: Inequalities and the YouTube algorithm. *Convergence*, 24(1): 69–84.

Bolin, G. (2012) 'The labour of media use', *Information, Communication & Society* 15 (6): 796–814.

Bucher, M. and Shannon, M. (2020) 'Behind the Scenes of a Tik Tok Vidoe: Weeks of work for a second of content' *Wall Street Journal*, November 14. https://www.wsj.com/story/behind-the-scenes-of-a-tiktok-video-weeks-of-work-for-seconds-of-content-b5d70cd0 (date accessed October 14 2023)

Cunningham, S. and Craig, D. (2019) *Social Media Entertainment: The New Intersection of Hollywood and Silicon Valley*. New York: New York University Press.

Dalla Costa, M. and James, S. (1972) *The Power of Women and the Subversion of the Community*. London: Falling Wall Press.

Davis, A.Y. (2019) *Women, Race & Class*. Penguin Modern Classics. London: Penguin Books.

De Kosnik, A. (2016). *Rogue Archives: Digital Cultural Memory and Media Fandom*. Cambridge, MA: MIT Press.

Dovey, J. (2000) *Freakshow: First Person Media and Factual Television*. London: Sterling, VA: Pluto Press.

Duffy, B.E. (2016) 'The romance of work: Gender and aspirational labour in the digital culture industries', *International Journal of Cultural Studies* 19 (4): 441–457.

Duffy, B.E. (2017) *On (Not) Getting Paid to Do What You Love: Gender, Social Media and Aspirational Work*. New Haven, CT and London: Yale University Press.

Federici, S. (2004) *Caliban and the Witch: Women, the Body and Primitive Accumulation*. New York: Autonomedia.

Fisher, E. (2015) '"You Media": Audienceing as marketing in social media', *Media, Culture and Society* 37 (1): 50–67.

Fuchs, C. (2011a) 'An alternative view of privacy on Facebook', *Information* 2: 140–165.

Fuchs, C. (2011b) 'Web 2.0, prosumption, and surveillance', *Surveillance and Society* 8 (3): 288–309.

Giddens, A. (1991) *Modernity and Self Identity*. Cambridge: Polity.

Gill, R. (2011) '"Life as a Pitch": Managing the self in new media work', in Deuze, M. (ed.) *Managing Media Work*. London: Sage, pp. 249–262.

Goggin, J. (2018) '"How do those Danish Bastards sleep at night?"*: Fan labor and the power of cuteness', *Games and Culture* 13 (7): 747–764.

Griffen-Foley, B. (2004) 'From tit-bits to big brother: A century of audience participation in the media', *Media, Culture and Society* 26 (4): 533–548.

Hearn, A. (2008) 'Variations on the branded self: Theme, invention, improvisation and inventory', in Hesmondhalgh, D. and Toynbee, J. (eds.) *The Media and Social Theory*. London: Routledge, pp. 194–210.

Hesmondhalgh, D. (2010) 'User-generated content, Free Labour and the Cultural Industries', *ephemera* 10 (3.4): 267–284.

Hill, A. (2005) *Reality TV: Audiences and Popular Factual Television*. London: Routledge.

Horton, R. and Wohl, D. (1956) 'Mass communication and para-social interaction: Observations on intimacy at a distance', *Psychiatry* 19 (3): 215–229.

Jarrett, K. (2008) 'Laundering women's history, a feminist critique of the social factory', *First Monday* 22 (3): online.

Jarrett, K. (2014) 'The relevance of "women's work"', *Television & New Media* 15(1): 14–29.

Jarrett, K. (2016) *Feminism, Labour and Digital Media: The Digital Housewife*. London and New York: Routledge.

Jarrett, K. (2022) *Digital Labour*. London: Polity.

Jhally, S. and Livant, B. (1986) 'Watching as working: The valorization of audience consciousness', *Journal of Communication* 36 (3): 124–143.

Lazzarato, M. (1996) 'Immaterial labour', in Hardt, M. and Virno, P. (eds.) *Radical Thought in Italy: A Potential Politics*, Minneapolis, University of Minnesota Press.

Marwick, A. (2013) *Status Update: Celebrity, Publicity and Branding in the Social Media Age*. Haven, CT: Yale University Press.

Marx, K. (1939/1993) *Grundrisse. Foundations of the Critique of Political Economy*. London: Penguin Books.

Meehan, E. (2013) 'Gendering the commodity audience: Critical media research, feminism, and political economy', in Durham, M.G. and Kellner, D.M. (eds.) *Media and Cultural Studies*. Malden, MA: Blackwell, pp. 311–321.

Neff, G., Wissinger, E., Zukin, S. (2005) 'Entrepreneurial labor among cultural producers: 'Cool' jobs in 'hot' industries', *Social Semiotics* 15(3): 307–334.

Noble, S.U. (2018) *Algorithms of Oppression How Search Engines Reinforce Racism*. New York: New York University Press.

Ouellette, L. and Hay, J. (2008) *Better Living Through Reality TV: Television and Post-welfare citizenship*. Malden, MA: Wiley-Blackwell.

Pham, M.T. (2015) *Asians Where Clothes on the Internet: Race, Gender and the Work of Personal Style Blogging*. Durham, NC and London: Duke University Press.

Proctor, J. (2021) 'Labour of love: Fan labour, BTS, and South Korean Soft Power', *Asia Marketing Journal* 22. https://doi.org/10.53728/2765-6500.1369.

Raphael, C. (2009) 'The political economic origins of Reali-TV', in Murray, S. and Ouellette, L. (eds.) *Reality TV Remaking Television Culture* (2nd ed.). New York: New York University Press, pp. 123–140.

Ross, A. (2009) *Nice Work If You Can Get It: Life and Labor in Precarious Times*. New York: New York University.

Scott, S. (2015) '"Cosplay is serious business": Gendering material fan labor on "heroes of cosplay"', *Cinema Journal* 54 (3): 146–154.

WORK **139**

Senft, T. (2008) *Camgirls: Celebrity and Community in the Age of Social Media*. New York: Peter Lang.

Skeggs, B. and Wood, H. (2012) *Reacting to Reality TV: Audience, Performance, Value*. London: Routledge.

Skeggs, B. and Yuill, S. (2019) 'Subjects of value and digital personas: Reshaping the bourgeois subject, unhinging property from personhood', *Subjectivity* 12: 82–99.

Smythe, D. (1977) 'Communications: Blindspot of Wester Marxism', *Canadian Journal of Political and Social Theory/Revue canadienne de theorie politique etsociale* 1 (3): 1–28.

Strathern, M. (1992) *After Nature: English Kinship in the late Tentieth Century*. Cambridge: Cambridge University Press.

Stanfill, M. (2019) *Exploiting Fandom: How the Media Industry Seeks to Manipulate Fans*. Chicago, IL: University of Iowa Press.

Taylor, C. (1989) *Sources of the Self: The Making of the Modern Identity*. Cambridge: Cambridge University Press.

Taylor, C. (1991) *The Ethics of Authenticity*. Cambridge: Cambridge University Press.

Terranova, T. (2000) 'Free labor: Producing culture for the digital economy', *Social Text* 18 (2): 33–58.

Tuchman, G. (1978) 'Introduction: The symbolic annihilation of women by the mass media', in Tuchman, G., Kaplan, D.A., and Benet, J. (eds.) Hearth and Home: Images of Women in the Mass Media. New York: Oxford University Press, pp. 3–38.

Weber, B. (2009) *Makeover TV: Selfhood, Citizenship and Celebrity*. Durham, NC: Dule University Press.

Wernick, A. (1991) *Promotional Culture*. London and Thousand Oaks, CA: Sage.

Wissinger, E. (2015) '#NoFilter: models, glamour labor, and the age of the blink', (In: Davis J, Jurgenson N (eds) Theorizing the Web 2014). *Interface* 1(1): 1–20. Available at: https://www.academia.edu/20536708/_Nofilter_Models_Glamour_Labor_and_the_Age_of_the_Blink

Wood, H. (2009) *Talking with Television: Women, Television and Modern Self-reflexivity*. Urbana, IL: University of Illinois Press.

Wood, H. (2017) 'Performing the self in the media - talk shows and reality television', in L. Van Zoonen (ed.) *International Encyclopedia of Media Effects*. Oxford: Wiley.

Wright, E.O. (1997) *Class Counts: Comparative Studies in Class Analysis*. Cambridge: Cambridge University Press.

6

THE DIGITAL CIRCUIT

SCENARIO: YOU DO THE WORK.

In this chapter, rather than open with a scenario, I am going to ask you, reader, to come up with your own. I am going to ask you to do the work. I want you to keep in mind a few sensitising issues from the various chapters in this book – that is, the overarching ideas about media change with which audiences are figured (Chapter 1). In Chapter 2, we discussed how we have arrived in a digitised environment, through following a history of media transformations that laid the ground for our current socio-cultural moment. There are 'anchors' in older media forms, practices and engagements that we should remember, as well as being alert to those which are newly emerging. In Chapter 3, We have understood the importance of issues of 'meaning' in order to interrogate just how it is that a culture operates with its own understandings and political motivations, and how these are central to considering the work audiences do in interpreting media. In Chapter 3, we also understood 'making-meaning' as not just a linguistic process, but a broader one that can also involve certain questions of 'use' and 'form' which continue to be valuable in a more participatory context. Fourth, In Chapter 4, we thought about feelings

DOI: 10.4324/9781003414575-7

THE DIGITAL CIRCUIT **141**

and the ways in which they can ignite audience creativity (including fandom), as well as give signals to newly emergent sentiments and moods from the ground – online or offline – which are tied to culturally-specific shifts. And finally, in Chapter 5, we discussed how audience engagements can be characterised as 'work' because they produce material which continues to accrue profits for capitalism, and now platform capitalism; and we reflected on the considerations of the audience as commodity in the rise and extension of the cultural industries. Each of these aspects (and they are by no means finite), are useful for a conjunctural analysis of the present digital landscape.

As you enter into this final chapter, I want you to think of a scenario of your own, a personal one. Come up with one digitised activity that you undertake regularly (selfies, meme generation, Instagram curating, Twitch streaming, social media chat, TV streaming, etc.). It can involve a substantial commitment or it can be something you consider banal, ritualised and part of the everyday. I want you to work with some of the ideas here and ask yourself, what does this personal activity tell you about everything else? In other words, what can it tell you about the current conjunctural moment?

QUESTION: HOW SHOULD WE ADOPT AN 'AUDIENCE-SENSITIVE' APPROACH TO DIGITAL CULTURE FOR CULTURAL STUDIES?

In this final chapter, I draw some of the threads of this book together and argue for extending notions of audiencing into the digital age for the ongoing project of Cultural Studies. In Chapter 1 of this book, we discussed some of the transformations in media that we now must take into account, depending upon their geo-political location: audiences are mediatised; audiences are (mostly) neoliberal; audiences are workers; and audiences are data - all of which are based upon who and where we are, because experiences are geographically and socially contingent. However, we are always still the 'warm bodies' through which our cultural practices are formed, lived and experienced. The Cultural Studies project of audience analysis has always been about the workings of power and a commitment to how it is that lived experience is influenced by – but also struggles with

142 THE DIGITAL CIRCUIT

and against – dominating forces. Beginning from the premise that we need to to consider the workings of culture in any hegemonic project, Cultural Studies allows us room to interrogate the reception of dominant media messages, at the same time as it opened up space for 'resistive' (Chapter 3) or perhaps 'emergent' sentiments and ideas (Chapter 4). These most basic of tenets are not completely outmoded since at a time of the consistent legitimising of consent for rampant social inequality, our commitment to interrogating ideology must surely be more robust than ever (Downey et al., 2014). However, it is also clear that that we need to take into account the transformative effects of our ongoing embedding within mediated structures that offer up some challenges to our analysis of representational regimes.

Here I will recap some of the developments in media that make audience analysis even more complex but no less important. Technological developments do of course present alternative engagements and audience activities that are continually changing, so much so that it is hard to keep up. We need to keep pace with these changes, but we also need to hold on to our sense of historical development as well as our sense of 'conjunctural critique' (Chapter 1). Some of the developments in media studies that have tried to keep pace with change have sometimes stymied a sense of contextual critique – 'critique' I think of as an understanding of what audience activities, interpretations, and moods tells us about any particular moment in time or conjuncture. For instance, increased use of economistic metaphors and the accounts of datafication seem to obscure our analysis of 'ordinary' audiences and users in the field. In this chapter, we will discuss how the practices of audiencing are involved across cultural processes; we will attend to specific contingencies of the moment – and we will use some of Annette Hill and Peter Dalgren's (2023) ideas to analyse media engagements. We will also revisit the classic 'circuit of culture' (DuGay et al., 1997, 2013) and think about how we might locate audiences at the heart of a digital circuit and across its cultural processes. My argument is that the cultural circuit always needed another dimension for thinking through the precise way people engage with media. Its development from the encoding/decoding model has always relied too heavily on textual ideas of representation derived from a linguistic model. In the digital environment we are faced with multiple and dynamic forms of engagement (across production and consumption). My argument is that by adding another dimension to the cultural circuit that attends to *form* (see Chapter 3), we can approach audiencing in the digital age in a way that attends to the current complex techno-social formations and practices of audiences. This will allow us a fully conjunctural critique of the audience that extends the arguments for a Cultural Studies audience project that I have described in this book.

AUDIENCES ARE INDUSTRIOUS

In their introduction to the text *Creator Culture,* Cunningham and Craig (2021: 4) suggest that, 'as industries and cultures change, so fields of study need to change'. They are talking about approaches to the media industries and the way they are challenged by the formation of a whole new social media entertainment industry, but I would also add that one of the evolving changes at the heart of these developments is the relationship to audiences and audiencing. Whilst the moving boundaries between production and consumption led to the generation of a new category of 'prosumer' (Bruns, 2009) and a consideration of whether we are all produsers now (Bird, 2011), such conflations barely seem to address how our interaction with digital platforms encourages a plethora of modes of engagement. These range from fleeting 'likes' to 'doom-scrolling', to perhaps more sustained engagement in downloading Netflix series' or recreating Manga animation. Many of us – with connectivity that is – engage with an extending number of websites, mobile apps, platforms, and actively do things like generate GIFs, memes, videos, in relationships which all the time involve producing, consuming, sharing and communicating. These engagements maintain and establish relationships: with traditional media industries, with affective communities of likeminded individuals, with content creators across various platforms, with selves and avatars, as well as para-social encounters with multiple immediate and distant others. All of these engagements are constantly evolving at a dramatic pace and they are at the heart of how culture is formed: how we make culture out of the conditions of our existence on the ground. As Sarah Kember and Joanna Zylinska (2012: 13) argued 'It is not simply the case that 'we' – that is autonomously existing humans – live in a complex technological environment that we can manage, control and 'use'. Rather that we are

144 THE DIGITAL CIRCUIT

physically and ontologically part of that environment, and it makes no more sense to talk of us using it than it does of it using us.' We are therefore, as audiences, constantly mutually reproducing a digital environment characterised by rapid change as well as by unequal power relations.

What kind of a role do we play in this immersive environment and how can we understand what this means for our critique of the current conjuncture? As Nitin Govil (2013: 176) argued about the developments in the media industries, 'we need to broaden the range of practices that count as industrial' with a 'more dynamic sense of industries as social and textual arrangements'. So too we need to broaden the range of practices that count as 'audiencing' as they engage with technological and industrial arrangements. Indeed, in a digital participatory context, the textual, social and technological overlap and are mutually productive of one another in a very dynamic sense.

To take one example, *all* communication through our presentation of self involves a sense of audience – the person to whom we are addressing and speaking in 'impression management' (Goffman, 1959). Across our actions on blogs, websites, mobile apps, and social media we are presenting a version of ourselves that requires us to consciously practice curating a self in relation to others, see for instance Chapter 5 and our discussion of 'micro-celebrity' (Senft, 2008). As Boyd and Marwick (2011) describe from the broadcast media to networked media, the trajectory of an 'imagined audience' becomes even more complex: 'The networked audience contains many different social relationships to be navigated, so users acknowledge concurrent multiple audiences. Just as writers fictionalize the audience within the text in their audience addressed, Twitter users speak directly to their imagined audience' (2011: 130).

Orienting oneself to an 'imagined audience' therefore becomes very much part of the contemporary technological environment in ways that can tell us something about the current moment. We have to take this into account for audience analysis. Memes, for instance, encourage purposeful interaction and involve a directional intention. They often use oppositional elements to address particular publics in a process that simultaneously engages production and consumption and through which new meanings are generated (Wiggins, 2019). Wiggins refers to interactions with memes as 'micro-activism', and

THE DIGITAL CIRCUIT 145

it has popularly been referred as 'slacktivism' for the effects of the appropriation of lazy click-throughs and likes. But as Denisova (2019) demonstrates, in the political context of Russia, meme generation can also form part of the battleground between state propaganda and political resistance. Such is the industriousness of audiences that practices sometimes blur the lines of professional and amateur production, as we discussed in Chapter 5. Crystal Abidin (2020) even uses the phrase 'meme factories' to talk about the 'work' involved in meme curation during the recent Covid pandemic.

In Chapter 5's discussion about understanding audience activities as work, we began to see how platforms engage 'users' in a range of strategies to enhance their visibility, adopt processes of self-optimisation, or embark in operational tactics against the algorithmic certainties which evade them. There is increasingly a process whereby content creators are 'professionalised' as 'videographers, editors, on-screen talent, brand ambassadors, merchandise producers, marketers, and PR Reps, and they must find ways to monetize their content if they wish to sustain careers in SME' (Glatt and Banet-Weiser, 2021: 45). Audiencing therefore also begins to involve the increasing adoption of professional activities by amateurs that were once contained within the realm of the media industries and production. Audiencing is not just watching.

Audiences are therefore 'industrious' and industrialising in their tactics, but many analyses of influencers seem to agree that this is not an even playing field, and that some can more easily 'strategise' for commercial advantage (mostly white, cis-gendered, middle-class, able-bodied women) than others, in a highly competitive business (Bishop, 2018; Khaled, 2019; Glatt, 2023). Here it seems that the symbolic struggle is one over annihilation – it is a struggle with and against the algorithm for visibility itself. Audiences are therefore actively involved in the gamification of their own visibility and terms of representation. In accounts of engagements with digital culture there is often a slippage between the terms user/audience; for some, 'user' entirely supplants the term audience in the digital landscape. But the user must always be conscious of their own orientation towards an audience, and so audiencing is very much a dialectic process as we are embedded in circuits of digital culture involved in simultaneous processes of production and consumption.

146 THE DIGITAL CIRCUIT

AUDIENCE ENGAGEMENTS

The key challenge for the audience researcher in the contemporary environment is dealing with this hyper-complexity in densely mediated societies. The digital environment is like a set of moving sands into which new formations, apps, platforms, user/audience behaviour is continuously emerging and changing shape. Popular attempts to characterise the digital environment as a stable entity that is toxic, distracting us and destroying our sociality, can only be met empirically with a series of ambiguities through which digital formations can be the cure to some social ills, at the same time as they can generate new ones (Paasonen, 2021).

Peter Dahlgren and Annette Hill (2023) have recently given us a helpful road map to think about media engagement in the digital environment. 'Engagement' is a term that has often surfaced throughout this book and it is helpful for the ways in which it centres social *practices* with media, foregrounding activities that can stretch across multiple contexts and conditions. Dahlgren and Hall (2023) suggest that media engagement 'is a spectrum of phenomena that is processual and protean; it is a shape-changer' (2023: 25). This point about shape-changing is important and one that we need to carry forward into any audience analysis – the sense that all the conditions we describe will only exist for a particular moment in time in an ever-evolving set of circumstances.

Dalgren and Hill (2023) therefore suggest that we attend to five parameters: context, motivations, modalities, intensities and consequences. The interlocking and fluid nature of these parameters is set out like a railroad map each flowing into one another to give a sense of constant movement and change. 'Contexts' refers to the major societal conditions in which any engagement occurs: they can refer to the broader structures of neoliberalism or economic crises, for instance. 'Motivations' refers to a sense of intentionality behind the engagement, and reflects questions of gratifications that can take into account curiosity or information-seeking for instance (Chapter 3). 'Intensities' have to do with the emotional force of an engagement or questions of length and duration that echo some of our concerns about feeling in Chapter 4. 'Consequencies' refers to any outcomes of the engagement that can be predicted or unforeseen – it could be a sense

THE DIGITAL CIRCUIT **147**

of empowerment or pleasure – although of course these may seem to overlap with other parameters.

The remaining perameter, 'modalities' is the one that I want to highlight and make a strong case for in the future of audience research. If you recall in Chapter 1, Nico Carpentier (2014) suggests that it is the modalities of audience engagements that are novel in a participatory context, over and above anything else. Modalities refer to the 'communicative character of that on which the engagement builds' (Dahlgren and Hill, 2023: 30). 'Modality' and 'form' are related terms which come from discourse and literary analysis: 'Form' tends to refer to the overall structure and shape of a text or discourse, whilst 'mode' can refer to some kind of intention in terms of a relationship with an audience – argumentation, or rhetoric for instance. These are important terms for media studies dealing with hypercomplexity. If you recall in Chapter 3, we discussed how attention to form can help us to focus on medium-specificity: on the ways in which any medium enables and generates particular engagements with audiences as opposed to attending only to 'content'. Form is the 'mode in which a thing... manifests itself' (Corner, 2011: 50) and it opens up our analysis to questions of aesthetics, genre and style, at the same time that thinking about 'mode' or 'modality' can refer to the technical infrastructures through which we come into contact with media – for instance, the storyworlds in transmedia environments through which audiences navigate platforms and worlds. (Evans, 2019).

Platforms equally require attention to form. In the article 'the interface as discourse', Mel Stanfill (2015) describes how interfaces can produce common-sense norms through which users are encouraged to act. Work on affordances and interfaces discusses the cultural work that software can do in both reinforcing hegemonic norms and providing spaces to undermine them. Victoria Simon (2020) also discusses the user interface design of music apps – ThumbJam, iMaschine 2 and Skram – which inscribe normative ideas of what she calls 'human perfectability'. Work on the emergence of health apps discusses how participants' actions help to change and develop the infrastructure itself in a process they describe as 'athletic':

> Critical accounts of digital media platforms then need to focus not only on how we 'narrate' our experience, but also the role we play in

148 THE DIGITAL CIRCUIT

> 'programming' the infrastructure that is used to experiment with social reality, our minds, and our bodies.

(2020: 529)

Kruger and Spilge (2019) in their analysis of the dating app Tinder discuss the ways in which features such as swiping right help to cement a commodified and gaming approach to dating, whilst at the same time they suggest that there is sentient recourse to 'gut instinct' which seems to run counter to the overarching framework. Their example relies on their own auto-ethnographic walk through of the app – whilst the other examples rely on a reading of the app design and interviews with designers. Interfaces can, therefore, set the parameters for engagement.

For the purposes of this chapter, I am going to stay with the term 'form' because it can, following Corner, capture orientations towards the audience. It can help us to understand just *how* audiences 'get it' and understand what they should do to engage in/with media. For a Cultural Studies approach however, we cannot make assumptions about what audiences do solely based on our own analysis of form, we also need to understand how they are lived and used, we also need to understand those 'warm bodies' that we discussed in Chapter 1, as they come into contact with any mediated interface.

WHERE ARE THE PEOPLE?

As we discussed in Chapter 1, it is tempting to read audiences through the data generated by platforms to know what they are doing online. Processes of automation that record and classify our preferences offer the audience up as an informational commodity through a heady combination of 'numerology and alchemy' in the information age whereby predicting audience behaviour has become a commercially lucrative pursuit (Athique, 2018). Whilst these tools may offer the audience researcher some new potential, as Adrian Athique cautions, we need to remember that audiences are NOT data. This is reminiscent of Ien Ang's (1990) call to understand the complexity of the television audience, against the dominance of the measurement perspectives of the ratings industry. Others have argued that audience studies needs to continue to counter some of these data-led trends. For instance, in

THE DIGITAL CIRCUIT **149**

their agenda for the future of audience research, Brit Ytre-Arne and Ranjana Das (2018) suggest that:

> Across the priorities, we argue for contextualised, critical research into everyday encounters with intrusive and algorithmic interfaces, over-coming a range of limitations of large-scale big data approaches (c.f. boyd and Crawford 2013), reasserting normative ambitions behind holding media institutions accountable for fairer outcomes for audiences in datafied societies, *and* carrying into this task the close to seventy-five years of research into audiences' experiences as readers, listeners, viewers, fans, subcultures, users and publics and other over-lapping categories.
>
> (2018: 186 my emphasis)

I wholly agree with these propositions as vital to the current conjuncture where, according to Couldry and van Dijck (2015) 'Calling an algorithmically defined online configuration "social," has been one of the smartest semantic moves in the history of media institutions' (2015: 3).

As we mentioned in Chapter 1, Sonia Livingstone (2019) argued that in media studies' recent, legitimate, concerns over the reach and power of the big global tech companies, the emphasis upon data-processing power and the 'mediatisation' of everything, has led to the downplaying of audience research and the significance of the 'life-world'. We can learn our lessons from the history of research into audience effects where macro-fears about passive and manipulated audiences are often complicated by critical research on the ground, as we also saw in Chapter 2. In response to this, Livingstone (2019: 178) suggests, 'I can only urge attention to the whole circuit of culture, including regulation'.

However, there has been a kind of taken-for-grantedness about what the 'circuit of culture' means as a shorthand for a more Cultural Studies approach to media research per se. The circuit, as derived by Paul Du Gay and Stuart Hall (1997/2013) and colleagues at the Open University, describes how a cultural artefact passes through various cultural processes, which, in combination, are articulated to become meaningful in any given society. For audience research we must take into account the way audiences are social and embedded in history,

150 THE DIGITAL CIRCUIT

but this must also refer to a conjunctural understanding of the here and now that insists upon critique. As Nick Couldry (2020) has argued in relation to some of the philosophical trends that have held sway in the social sciences to account for datafication, we need to move away from descriptivism and recover a critique of the social order. This relies on a moral challenge for critical theory and one which confronts capitalism's tendencies towards totalising frameworks and its limitations upon human capacities: 'To register this, we surely need less descriptivism and more concern with the actual constraints on human agency and their consequences for the quality of human life' (2020: 1146). Any return to the circuit of culture must therefore do so with a strong sense of the critical project of Cultural Studies at its centre, and not with a will simply to endlessly describe the potential and shifting range of engagements and activities that abound in contemporary media culture.

THE DIGITAL CIRCUIT

In the introduction to the second edition of *Doing Cultural Studies* (2013) Du Gay and Madsen reflect on how odd it has been for (what they describe as) a modest textbook account of culture to have been so hotly tested and debated. In the spirit of updating their textbook account, I offer a similar adoption of the circuit of culture model to encourage students to apply a Cultural Studies approach to audiences in the contemporary digital conjuncture. There are a number of things to consider when returning to the circuit of culture for the future of audience research. The first and most basic is that its inception was derived before many of the complications of participatory media, and in that way it speaks to more stable models of audience analysis. The circuit of culture was developed from Stuart Hall's (1980) 'encoding/decoding' model which set out his ideas that meanings were not transmitted in a linear fashion but are part of a more dynamic (semiological) process; these ideas were later tested in David Morley's (1980) *The Nationwide Audience* (Chapter 3). There was, however, an earlier model of the circuit by Richard Johnson (1986) through which he offered a heuristic account of the circulation of culture in order to reach beyond contemporaneous overly economistic (Marxist) models where culture is determined entirely by the mode of production. In the

THE DIGITAL CIRCUIT **151**

later model, by Du Gay et al. (1997, 2013), we can see five major cultural processes: representation, identity, production, consumption, and regulation. 'Taken together, they complete a sort of circuit – what we term the 'circuit of culture' – through which any analysis of a cultural artefact must pass if it is to be adequately studied.' (Du Gay et al., 2013: xxx). It is important to note how each of the cultural processes articulate with one another – they are not, and they never were, separated entities.

Most important to note is that the circuit was designed with the cultural artefact at the centre. Du Gay et al.'s (1997) study discusses the Sony Walkman where they suggest, 'one should at least explore how it is represented, what social identities are associated with it, how it is produced and consumed, and what mechanisms regulate its distribution and use' (Du Gay et al., 2013: xxx). Similarly, Johnson's model was illustrated by the use of the car, the Mini Metro, through which consumption, labour relations of the time, and British culture could be read. The circuit of culture then lends itself most easily to the 'biography of the cultural artefact' where audiences are conjured in relation to consumption, identity, and in Johnson's model, to 'lived experience'. In Du Gay et al. (1997) the audiences of the Walkman were discussed by reference to Ray Chow's (1993) analysis of the use of the Walkman in China. There, its use in public allows young people to drown out the noise of the Chinese state, demonstrating that we cannot assume the meanings of use from Sony's intentions, or impose a dominant interpretation of use, onto a specific geographical context.

Du Gay et al.'s (2013) second edition of *Doing Cultural Studies* goes some way into exploring whether the circuit is still useful for a digital environment. Their key issues were:

i   the evolving boundaries of the public and the private as a basis for regulation – for instance the nature of privacy in processes of data surveillance,
ii the ongoing interrelation of production, consumption and identity – although it is important to note that this feature was also at the centre of the original model preceding ideas of the 'prosumer',
iii representation in the digital world – which was given some primacy in the original model as it aimed to challenge ideas that culture was entirely determined by economic activity, as

'all economically relevant activity is culturally constituted in important parts' (2013: xxiii).

The extensive complex interrelationships between production, consumption and identity are of course an ongoing source of exploration for any commitment to audience studies. Others have argued that the notion of circuitry is still useful for digital culture (Bødker, 2016). Henry Bødker's analysis of circuits of contemporary journalism reminds us that 'Hall sees circulation as both technological and hermeneutical processes through which meaning and/or ideology move into and out of discursive form' (2016: 409). In digital culture, processes of meaning-making are merging with the circulation of the commodity form – a simple 'click' or 'like' for instance can make that commodity available to someone else, in a new moment of consumption, circulation and distribution. In these ways audiences are consuming others' consumption at the same time as they are augmenting commodities – adding to them, re-energising them, generating new forms of value from them. How can we account for this within the cultural circuit?

What we need, according to Bødker (2015), is not just an account of the circulation of meaning, but also the meaning of circulation. I would add that we also need an extended idea of how meaning is generated beyond the discursive – to include, as we have discussed in this book, meaning in relation to *form*, including relations like affect. One of the limitations of the cultural circuit is its derivation from the encoding/decoding model that privileges the linguistic formation of meaning, which we argued in Chapter 3 cannot fully account for how all media products become meaningful. (See also, Wood, 2007, 2009). In Bødker's account of that model he draws out how in Hall's original analysis of television, 'while the technological and material aspects, or the TV as medium, are seen as integral to the encoding process, these somehow disappear in the conceptualization of the distribution and decoding process, which is mainly talked about in linguistic terms' (2016: 416). Whilst Hall could not have foreseen how audiences now leave the digital traces of their participation online, it still leaves out the important questions of 'form' as we have discussed above.

Richard Johnson's (1986) earlier model of the circuit did account for 'form' in his diagram, but it is located outside of other processes

THE DIGITAL CIRCUIT 153

and attached only to the notion of texts. We can presume that this refers to more aesthetic features and related to questions of genre and style. In his account, he was trying to reconcile the then competing distinctions between culturalist and structuralist traditions in early Cultural Studies, which he finds an unhelpful separation. 'Nor are the consumers of cultural forms formally or regularly distinguished from their producers, or far removed from them in time or space' (Johnson, 1986: 51). As discussed above and in Chapter 3, Corner's (2011) attention to form considers how formal features are 'apprehended' by their audience. Therefore for us, by re-centring form as a more central cultural process it gives us a sense of how the structure of a cultural artefact (which can include features such as narrative style and genre as well as platforms, architectures and interfaces) become deeply entwined into the contexts of their occasion on the ground. (As we have seen in this book questions of genre and style in relation to talk television's communicative address or reality television's production of immediacy and intimacy are vitally important to the ways in which audiences are encouraged to engage, make-meaning and feel (Wood, 2009; Skeggs and Wood, 2012; Chapters 3 and 4).)

The cultural circuit has always needed another dimension, but my argument here is that this extra dimension of 'form' can become more central to the ongoing dynamic relations of production, consumption and identity. This is now pressing in the current conjuncture whereby variations in online platform architectures delimit the very terms of our engagements. The de-centralised online ecosystem of the World Wide Web in the 1990s that held so much radical potential, has now been supplanted by the emergence of dominating platforms which run their own closed quasi-operating systems. Platforms therefore become powerful, 'cultural shapers', they

> play a major role in governing the forms of creativity and social inter-action that take place through them. They set rules about what content and behaviour are allowed, even amplified, and what content and behaviour are not allowed and discouraged.
>
> (Burgess, 2021: 24)

For Ted Striphas (2015) in his discussion of 'algorithmic culture' the algorithmic precedents which sort, classify and hierarchise people, places, objects and ideas are making the big platforms like Amazon, Google and Facebook, 'the new apostles of culture' which beget new algorithmic forms of oppression (Noble, 2018; Benjamin, 2019). This may seem an entirely closed loop whereby the conditions of media power are all encompassing, but if we want to understand the formation of this power and have any hope of challenging it, then we need to adopt an approach to audiences, with the 'warm bodies', to critique the domination of platform architectures.

One of the problems applying the circuit of culture to cultural practices across current big platforms – Google and YouTube (owned by Alphabet), Whatsapp and Instagram (owned by Facebook) or in China WeChat (owned by Tencent) IQiyi (controlled by Baidu) or TikTok (owned by ByteDance) – is that it is almost impossible to know what is 'under the hood' of the algorithm. As we saw in Chapter 5 content by certain groups risks being marginalised and excluded by the nefarious operations of algorithmic logics. Recent calls for holding platforms to account for their actions such as the Facebook Analytica scandal[1] must obviously continue in challenging a regulatory framework that is struggling to keep step with the pace of change. As audience researchers, we must also robustly service those calls with critique of what platforms generate in terms of their affordances on the ground and how (following Livingstone 2019) regulatory frameworks exercise forms of power and control over our media engagements. What platforms, and for that matter all media technologies and forms, allow and invite people to do needs to be explored, taking on board forms of subordination as well as finding space for resistance. As Tania Bucher (2016) argues in her research on users' understanding and perceptions of algorithms in social media platforms, how users imagine and expect certain algorithmic affordances, affects how they approach these platforms. Bucher and Helmond (2017) therefore call for: 'the notion of a platform-sensitive framework [which] is meant to emphasize the specificity of platforms as a socio-technological environment that draw different users together and which orchestrate the relations between different platform users.' (Bucher and Helmond, 2017). I want to suggest that by simply opening out the cultural circuit more fully to questions of Form, we may be able to incorporate such an approach into the existing circuit of culture.

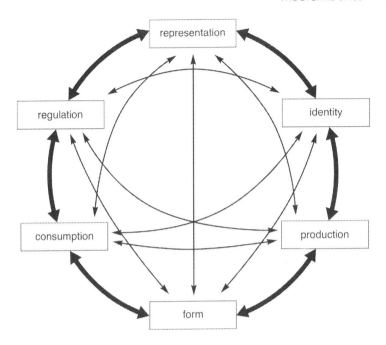

Figure 6.1 The digital circuit.

My suggestion is that for audience studies in the digital environment, we should insert Form as an important cultural process in between consumption and production. Form needs to be elevated as having a pivotal role in the understanding of culture, because it is at the heart of the way in which media architectures of all kinds develop overlapping engagements in which audiences are simultaneously producers and consumers. These might enable questions of use and algorithmic strategising with the platform but can also be 'articulated' with representations over symbolic struggles. This way the cultural circuit, and its necessary insistence on the free-flowing relationships between cultural processes, can be updated to more easily cope with the digital landscape. Any practice we look at might involve more than one circuit in a more layered approach to digital complexity, and any practice will need to deal with the complexities of consumption on the ground. It is important to do this so that questions of 'use' and 'affordance'

156 THE DIGITAL CIRCUIT

that characterise some studies of digital culture, can be adequately incorporated into the bigger question of, 'so what?' What difference does all of this make to the here and now? What difference does this make to the social order? Adding this dimension ensures that we avoid the traps of descriptivism and insists upon contextual critique.

KEEPING UP CONJUNCTURAL CRITIQUE: ARTICULATION

The key mechanism to apply the circuit of culture to our analysis is through the concept of 'articulation', which was central to the development of Cultural Studies' earlier methods and enabled a way to account for complexity whilst avoiding (class) reductionism or essentialism. For a longer account of the philosophical genealogies of theories of 'articulation' see Slack (1996), but for here it is important to understand that an analysis of a cultural practice requires an understanding of how the different elements – representation, identity, production, (now) form, consumption, and regulation – are articulated together in the generation of some kind of unity. It is not just that these things 'connect' but it is the very *process* of the creating of connections, of their dynamic interrelationships, that we must analyse, providing us with a 'complex structure' (Hall, 1980). As Jennifer Slack tells us:

> Interrogating any articulated structure or practice requires an examination of the ways in which the 'relatively autonomous' social, institutional, technical, economic, and political forces are organised into unities that are effective and relatively empowering or disempowering.
>
> (1996: 124)

This allows us a way to acknowledge movement and the ongoing *re*-articulation of contexts, 'the changing ensemble for forces (or articulations) that create and maintain identities that have real concrete effects' (Slack, 1996: 125) which need constant re-calibration in the fast-paced dynamism of digital culture.

These are the features of a 'conjunctural analysis', which as we have discussed require 'radical contextualisation' (Grossberg, 2010, Chapter 1). There should be a strong emphasis upon temporality, shaped by a need to understand 'what is going on now?', but it is not at all an ahistorical approach to analysis. In fact, it is precisely the

THE DIGITAL CIRCUIT **157**

opposite; it is a commitment to understanding exactly how the historical has helped to structure the present. How/why did we get here? An emphasis upon temporality is a call to *always* historicise which is often difficult for audience analysis when faced with a media field transforming at such a rapid pace that practices are quickly assigned as out of date. As Behrenshausen (2019) argues:

> The novel, the banal, and the reconfigured. The fresh, the stale, the remixed. Cultural Studies refuses the giveness of categories like these – refuses their claim to name mere epochs on a static and linear timeline – and addresses them instead as constructions germane to a particular arrangement of power-relations.
>
> (2019: 70)

This seems to echo Raymond Williams' (1961) critique of epochal periodisation in the discussion of the structure of feeling where the dominant, emergent and residual forms of culture reside together in the complex temporalities of any one moment in time (Chapter 4). I want to take a moment here to emphasise the 'radical' in Grossberg's formation. 'Radical' does not just refer to something as new, but rather as an adjective, 'as (especially of change or action) relating to or affecting the fundamental nature of something; *far-reaching or thorough.*' (OED my emphasis) This emphasis upon the depth of some particular action or change – its thoroughness – its scope – is something that we have to bring to our audience research.

THE PELOTON: A CONJUNCTURAL ANALYSIS

To conclude this chapter, and indeed conclude this book, I want now to return to the Peloton, the fitness bike user we began with in Chapter 1, to briefly illustrate how the cultural circuit was always at the heart of my thinking. And in the spirit of this book, I am going to centre the experience of the 'audience' rather than the cultural artefact of the bike, which I could also easily do. In fact, the audience for this particular example is me. Yes, the game is up, I purchased one during Covid lockdown.

To think about the audiences of the bike, I might generate a thought process like this:

158 THE DIGITAL CIRCUIT

PRODUCTION: Here, I could think about the marketing, apparel and design of the bike: how it is addressed to the ultimate middle-class consumer – who wants to prioritise their productivity and how that address is gendered. Peloton badly misjudged its audience when its Christmas advert of 2019 was judged to be sexist and patronising.[2] Peloton is owned by Peloton Interactive Inc. – an American company now with a range of interactive fitness equipment. Its current net-worth is around \$3.06 billion having received a spike in sales during Covid. The cost of the bike is immediately exclusionary as are the monthly payments. There is some, limited, open conflict on its social media sites which point to the exclusionary elements around certain forms of conspicuous consumption – like users keeping bikes in their 'quadruple garages'. Images of the bikes on cruise ships and 5* resorts, 'spotted' by users, shore-up the bikes' audiences and community as being mostly the elite. My relationship to the modes of production might involve an analysis of my own taking part in the enveloping 360 degree marketing strategy, across social media platforms, website discussions, boosting the content of the Instagram profiles of the fitness-instructor celebrities, and generating more digital traffic for the bike's brand. You could say I *work* for Peloton.

FORM: Here I could think about how I contribute to the algorithmic culture of the bike through the various interfaces, as it records and profiles my fitness scores and music preferences, generating and calculating data about me and trying to predict and inform my next move. The form of address combines para-social relationships with fitness instructors with a technological infrastructure. This includes the Peloton app, but also the user interface of the main screen on the bike through which I can see an instructor who 'shouts out' to me and I can mimic whilst I also track my progress and my heart rate. I wrestle with the interface of the bike's screen as I hide certain elements (affordances) that shame me – like the 'leaderboard' feature where you can see who is doing the same ride and who is ahead of you. There is more than one 'form' ' at work, on the bike and off the bike, in social media Facebook and Instagram Peloton accounts, which position me as part of a sociable yet highly competitive community and assume a kind of Pelo-identity

CONSUMPTION: Here, I can consider how I am part of the 172% increase in sales of the Peloton during the Covid pandemic of

THE DIGITAL CIRCUIT 159

2020. Lockdown created the perfect conditions for home fitness technologies and I was influenced by rules in the UK when outside exercise was limited to one hour per day. As part of that context, I am encouraged to consume the ideologies and the symbolic markers of the 'age of fitness' which is finely tuned to the workings of capitalism as part of the broader context for consumption. Jürgen Martschukat (2021) calls this a 'corporate fitness' in how it articulates a fitness for work and success. One popular addition to the bike is a laptop tray so that you can work and work-out simultaneously – something that I have easily avoided. I can therefore draw upon what the bike 'means' as a form of conspicuous consumption in an age of neoliberal, highly competitive, working and fitness culture, buying into the brand that is, 'empowering people to be the best version of themselves anywhere, anytime'[3].

REGULATION: Here, I should think about Peloton's privacy agreements, whilst I have to admit never reading them before I purchased. Who does? When you take a look, there is a description of these agreements to 'empower you', whilst at the same time acknowledging that, 'By using or submitting information through the Services, you are acknowledging the collection, transfer, manipulation, processing, storage, disclosure and other uses of your personal data as described in this Privacy Policy'[4]. I learn about all the personal information that I have provided to Peloton through the app including my image, my geo-location, my voice, and any user generated content on any of the associated sites. Then there is the information that is collected 'automatically', such as information collected through third-party applications such as Google Play or Appstore – or any third-party apps that I may have networked to the bike such as Strava or Fitbit. All of which I should be reassured is to 'better understand our members needs' – what a relief. But now I should think about how it is that my warm sweaty body is appropriated as 'data' and works to try and secure my ongoing attachment to the bike as part of the 'attention economy'.

REPRESENTATION: Here, I can think about how the whole bike is articulated across a model of representation that draws on familiar ideological tropes of a neoliberal work ethic through which working hard will be rewarded with success – these are reinforced by the number of before-and-after shots users post on the social

160 THE DIGITAL CIRCUIT

media communities. The bike's representational framework is simultaneously inclusionary and exclusionary. The fitness instructors are diverse (ethnically) though not in their bodily form – they are all of course fit, toned and conventionally beautiful and young. The themed rides take on elements of inclusion and tolerance such as Black Lives Matter week and Transawareness day – and during the awfulness of the pandemic, there were a number of workouts named 'resilience' rides that invited you to persevere and keep working – despite your failing mental health as part of the dominance of discourses of 'resilience' in anti-welfarist culture (McRobbie, 2020). We might say that the brand incorporates a kind of 'woke-washing' (Sobande, 2020) in that it speaks to you as a morally good, socially progressive and tolerant person, boosting your 'feel good' vibe generating affective attachments and encouraging you to 'live your best life'.

IDENTITY: Here I need to think about how each of these elements, articulated together, generate a sense of identity for the audience member/user with which I both do and do not feel comfortable – as the successful white and now middle-class working woman, my location in the Midlands of England, my age and my professional identity, make me the ideal consumer. I think about the way I use the app, choose the Electronic Dance Music but actually resist the appeals of the online communities to share stories about errant husbands, interiors and fashion. If I wanted to, I could join a community that share other cyclists' joys and attach a great deal of meaning to their the affective ties to one another as they form their own 'packs' and schedule rides at the same time. But my own reluctance to do so reveals the faultlines of the promoted subjectivity baked into the cultural forms and infrastructure of the bike against my own lived reality as a working single mother. I am almost the self-enterprising go-getting woman they require – but the bike is mostly dormant, mocking my failure from the corner of the bedroom, holding on to my clothes.

So what does the Peloton tell us about everything else? Of course this is not audience research, but an audience-sensitive approach to where we might begin and it requires much more empirical evidence with audiences on the ground (for an excellent discussion of how to approach the method of audience research, see Hermes and Kopitz, 2023). The rise of the cult of Peloton was occurring at a historical moment where rampant social inequalities were being laid bare by the Covid pandemic whilst the middle-classes were running away to the safety of their second homes (Kay and Wood, 2022). We should therefore explore what the work of a consumer 'cult' might do in order to distract and insulate its members from the harsh realities outside. What role are audience engagements with this complex digital cultural *form* playing in the extending conditions of social inequality? Ideological mechanisms are articulated across the circuit, through the interrelations between the elements of production, form, consumption, regulation, representation and identity which we might call a 'unity of insulation' that does considerable work on the ground.

If we think of the shape-changing nature of audience engagements, elements can shift and change like a kaleidoscope to form a particular pattern but when captured together we need to see the identify its particular unity and be alert to what it is telling us at any given moment in time. Just like the turning of the dial in a kaleidoscope will mean that the beads fall, shift and arrange themselves into new constellations, so too the contingent and contextual set of lived circumstances will re-organise the shape of media engagements alongside the evolution of platform architectures and mediated interfaces. But just because the shape is constantly evolving, it does not mean that it has no shape at all and we have to be alert to the precise formation of any conjunctural moment.

That is all from me. What does your example look like? How does your practice articulate around the digital circuit? Most importantly, for contextual critique, what is it telling you about everything else?

NOTES

1   https://www.nytimes.com/2018/04/04/us/politics/cambridge-analytica-scandal-fallout.html (date accessed October 18, 2023)
2   https://www.theguardian.com/media/2019/dec/04/peloton-backlash-sexist-dystopian-exercise-bike-christmas-advert (date accessed October 15, 2023).
3   https://www.onepeloton.co.uk/company (date accessed October 15, 2023).
4   https://www.onepeloton.co.uk/privacy-policy (date accessed October 15, 2023).

REFERENCES

Abidin, C. (2020) 'Meme factory cultures and content pivoting in Singapore and Malaysia during COVID-19', *Harvard Kennedy School Misinformation Review* 1 (3). https://doi.org/10.37016/mr-2020-031

162 THE DIGITAL CIRCUIT

Ang, I. (1990) *Desperately Seeking the Audience*. London: Routledge.

Athique, A. (2018) 'The dynamics and potentials of big data for audience research', *Media, Culture & Society* 40 (1): 59–74. https://doi-org.ezproxy.lancs.ac.uk/10.1177/0163443717693681

Behrenshausen, B. (2019) 'Cultural studies in the present tense'. *Cultural Studies*. 33: 68–74. https://doi.org/10.1080/09502386.2018.1543337

Benjamin, R. (2019) *Race after Technology: Abolitionist Tools for the New Jim Code*. Newark, NJ: Polity Press.

Bird, E. (2011) 'Are we all produsers now? Convergence and media audience practices', *Cultural Studies* 25 (4–5): 502–516.

Bishop, S. (2018) 'Anxiety, panic and self-optimisation: Inequalities in the YouTube algorithm', *Convergence* 24 (1): 69–84.

Bødker, H. (2015) 'Journalism as cultures of circulation', *Digital Journalism* 3 (1): 101–115. https://doi.org/10.1080/21670811.2014.928106

Bødker, H. (2016) 'Stuart Hall's encoding/decoding model and the circulation of journalism in the digital landscape', *Critical Studies in Media Communication* 33 (5): 409–423. https://doi.org/10.1080/15295036.2016.1227862

Bruns, A. (2009) 'From Prosumer to Produser: Understanding User-Led Content Creation'. Paper presented at Transforming Audiences Conference London September 2009. https://eprints.qut.edu.au/27370/

Bucher, T. (2016) 'The algorithmic imaginary: Exploring the ordinary affects of Facebook algorithms', *Information, Communication & Society* 20 (1): 1–15.

Bucher, T. and Helmond, A. (2017) 'The affordances of social media platforms', in Burgess, J., Poell, T., and Marwick, A. (eds.) *The SAGE Handbook of Social Media*. London and New York: SAGE Publications Ltd, pp. 233–253

Burgess, J. (2021) 'Platform studies', in Cunningham, S. and Craig, D. (eds.) *Creator Culture: An Introduction to Global Social Media Entertainment*. New York, NYU Press, pp. 21–38.

Dalgren, P. and Hill, A. (2023) *Media Engagement*. London: Routledge.

Carpentier, N. (2014) 'New configurations of the audience? The challenges of user generated content for audience theory and media participation', in Nightingale, V. (ed.) *The Handbook of Media Audiences*. Chichester: Wiley Blackman, pp. 190–212.

Chow, R. (1993) 'Listening otherwise, music miniaturized: a different kind of question about revolution', in During, S. (ed.) *The Cultural Studies Reader*. London: Routledge.

Couldry, N. (2020) 'Recovering critique in an age of datafication', *New Media and Society* 22 (7): 1135–1151.

Couldry, N. and van Dijck, J. (2015) 'Researching social media as if the social mattered', *Social Media + Society*, 1(2). https://doi.org/10.1177/2056305115604174

Corner, J. (2011) Theorising Media: Power, Form and Subjectivity Manchester, Manchester University Press.

Cunnungham, S. and Craig, D. (eds.) (2021) *Creator Culture: An Introduction to Global Social Media Entertainment*. New York: New York University Press.

THE DIGITAL CIRCUIT 163

Denisova, A. (2019) *Internet Memes and Society: Social, Cultural, and Political Contexts*. Routledge Advances in Internationalizing Media Studies. Milton: Taylor & Francis Group.

Downey, J., Titley, G., and Toynbee, J. (2014) 'Ideology critique: the challenge for media studies', *Media, Culture & Society*, 36(6): 878–887.

Evans, E. (2019) *Understanding Engagement in Transmedia Cultures*. London: Routledge.

Du Gay, P., et al. (1997/2013) *Doing Cultural Studies: The Story of the Sony Walkman*. London: Sage.

Glatt, Z. and Banet-Weiser, S. (2021) 'Productive ambivalence, economies of visibility, and the political potential of feminist YouTubers', in Cunningham, S. and Craig, D. (eds.) *Creator Culture: An Introduction to Social Media Entertainment*. New York: New York University Press, pp 39–56.

Glatt, Z. (2023) 'The intimacy triple bind: Structural inequalities and relational labour in the influencer industry', *European Journal of Cultural Studies*, online first. https://doi.org/10.1177/13675494231194156

Goffman, E. (1959) *The Presentation of Self in Everyday Life*. Garden City, NY: Doubleday.

Govil, N. (2013) 'Recognising "Industry"' Cinema Journal 52 (3): 172–176.

Grossberg, L. (2010) Cultural Studies in the Future Tense, Durham, Duke University Press.

Hall, S. (1980) 'Race, articulation and societies structured in dominance', in UNESCO (ed.) *Sociological Theories: Race and Colonialism*. Paris: UNESCO, pp. 305–345.

Hermes, J. and Kopitz, L. (2023) *The Pocketbook of Audience Research*. London: Routledge.

Johnson R. (1986) 'What is cultural studies anyway?', *Social Text* 6: 38–80.

Kay, J and Wood, H. (2022) 'The race for space': capitalism, the country and the city in Britain under COVID-19, *Continuum* 36 (2): 274–288.

Kember, S. and Zylinska, J. (2012) *Life after Media: Mediation as a Vital Process*. Cambridge, MA: MIT Press.

Khaled, A. (2019) 'A history of YouTube undermining its LGBT+ creators', *Medium*, June 5. Available at: http://medium.com

Krüger, S. and Spilde, A. (2019) 'Judging books by their covers – Tinder interface, usage and sociocultural implications', *Information, Communication & Society* 23: 1–16.

Livingstone, S. (2019) 'Audiences in an age of datafication: Critical questions for media research', *Television & New Media* 20 (2): 170–183.

Martschukat, J. (2021) *The Age of Fitness: How the Body came to Symbolise Success and Achievement*. London: Polity.

Marwick, A. E., and Boyd, D. (2011) 'I tweet honestly, I tweet passionately: Twitter users, context collapse, and the imagined audience', *New Media & Society*, 13(1): 114–133

McRobbie, A. 2020. *Feminism and the Politics of Resilience: Essays on Gender, Media and the End of Welfare*. Cambridge: Polity Press.

Morley, D. (1980) *The Nationwide Audience*. London: BFI.

Noble, S.U. (2018) *Algorithms of Oppression How Search Engines Reinforce Racism*. New York: New York University Press.

THE DIGITAL CIRCUIT

Paasonen, S. (2021) *Dependant, Distracted, Bored.* Cambridge, MA: MIT Press.

Senft, T. (2008) *Camgirls: Celebrity and Community in the Age of Social Media.* New York: Peter Lang.

Simon, V. (2020) 'Guided by delight: Music apps and the politics of user interface design in the IOS platform', *Television & New Media* 21(1): 60–74.

Skeggs, B. and Wood, H (2012) *Reacting to Reality Television: Audience, performance and value* London and New York: Routledge.

Slack, J.D. (1996) 'The theory and method of articulation in cultural studies', in D. Morley and K.H. Chen (eds.) *Critical Dialogues in Cultural Studies.* London and New York: Routledge, pp. 112–130.

Sobande, F. (2020) 'Woke-washing: "intersectional" femvertising and branding "woke" bravery', *European Journal of Marketing* 54 (11): 2723–2745.

Stanfill, M. (2015) 'The interface as discourse: The production of norms through web design', *New Media & Society* 17 (7): 1059–1074.

Striphas, T. (2015). 'Algorithmic culture'. *European Journal of Cultural Studies* 18(4–5): 395–412.

Wiggins, B. E. (2019) *The Discursive Power of Memes in the Digital Age.* New York: Routledge.

Williams, R. (1961) *The Long Revolution.* New York Chichester, West Sussex: Columbia University Press.

Wood, H. (2007) 'The mediated conversational floor: An interactive approach to audience reception analysis', *Media, Culture & Society* 29 (1): 75–103.

Wood, H. (2009) *Talking with Television: Women, Television and Modern self-reflexivity.* Urbana, IL: University of Illinois Press.

Ytre-Arne, B. and Das, R. (2018) 'An agenda in the interest of audiences: Facing the challenges of intrusive media technologies', *Television and New Media* 20 (2): 184–198.

INDEX

Note: *Italic* page numbers refer to figures and page numbers followed by "n" denote endnotes.

Abercrombie, Nicholas 2
Abidin, Crystal 129, 134, 145
active audience 6, 13, 16, 21, 22, 59, 68, 90; bad text *vs.* good audience 100; capitalism 21; cultural studies 63–66; fan activity 69; media audience 22; paradigm 66, 132; problem of 68–70; symbolic warfare 90; television 70; *see also* audiences
Adorno, Theodor 35, 36, 121
advanced economies 19
advertisement 121, 122, 130
affect/affective: communities 108; economies 98, 100; freedom 97, 100; labour 111, 127; performances 110; political mobilisation of 98; practice 102; publics 7, 87; theory of 99
Affect and Social Media (Ellis) 106
affective turn 7, 86, 87, 95–99
Ahmed, Sarah 98, 103, 105
algorithmic culture 110, 153, 158
algorithms 13, 22–24, 125, 133, 154
alien cultures 74
Alptekin, K. 90
Altheide, D.L. 13
Amazon 154
ambiguity 99, 105–106, 109
American Communication Studies 40
American culture, intimate public sphere 95
anchor 32, 34; audiences as workers 37; contemporary audience research 38; present media context 51
Andreessen, Marc 136n6
Andrejevic, Mark 97–98, 123, 126

An Everyday Magic (Kuhn) 46
Ang, Ien 3, 94, 110, 148
Anglo-American public life 39
Anselmo, D. W. 127
anthropology 66, 74, 76, 77
anti-fan dynamics 90, 108, 109
anti-racist diasporic groups 16–17
anti-welfareism 20
'anyone-as-someone' structures 72
Arab Spring 16, 107
articulation concept 26, 72, 108, 156
Athique, Adrian 22, 148
attention economy 20, 128, 159
audiences 2; attention economy 20; behaviour 41, 42, 70, 148; commodity 7, 120–122; conjunctural analysis 24–26; data 20; engagements 11, 15, 48, 146–148; experiences 44; free labour 22; industrious 143–145; labour theory 128; mass media 34; media production 14; mediatisation 12–13; motivations 75; neoliberal ideologies 19–20; 'para-social' relationship 42; as performers 122–124; sensitive approach 4, 5, 141; social life of 17; social media 106–109; sovereignty 37; symbolic warfare 90; taming of 34; theory 100; user-generated content 16; warm bodies 22–24; ways of seeing 33; work 119–120; workers 17–19; *see also individual entries*
auditorium 41
austerity culture 20
authentic human-social relations 18
auto-ethnographic walk 148

166 INDEX

Bandura, A. 43
Banet-Weiser, Sarah 127, 130
Barker, Martin 44, 70
BBC 15, 48, 51n2, 119, 127
Behrenshausen, B. 157
Benjamin, Walter 35
Bennett, T. 88
Berlant, Lauren 95
Black heterosexual audience 67
Black Women as Cultural Readers
    (Bobo) 66
Blumer, Herbert 40
Blumler, J.G. 71
'Bobo Doll' experiment 43
Bobo, Jacqueline 66
Bødker, Henry 152
Bodroghkozy, Aniko 90
Bolin, Goran 131, 135
Booth, Paul 69, 93
Bourdieu, Pierre 76, 87–88
Bourdon, Jerome 44, 45
Boyd, D. 144
brands 11; advertisement 122, 130;
    content creators 145; emotional
    investments 127; fan management
    93; influencers 42; relationships
    130; self-branding 127, 134–135;
    sponsorship 129; woke-washing 160
#BringBackOurGirls action 107
broader struggles 39
Brockley group 103, *104–105*, 111n7
Brown, J.R. 71
Bucher, Tania 23, 154
bullet theory 43
Butsche, Richard 32, 34, 37
ByteDance 126

Cantril, H. 41
capitalism 18, 21, 36, 95, 122, 133
Carpentier, Nico 16, 147
Castells, M. 16
Cavalcante, Andre 68, 98
celebrities 42, 123, 158
Centre for Contemporary Cultural
    Studies (CCCS) 63

Chatman, Dayna 108
Cheesman, M. 77
child-care resources 20
child protection 40
child psychology 40
China WeChat 154
Chow, Ray 151
cinema 33, 37, 39–41, 46
civilising mission 34
Clapham group 112n7
class: antagonism 35; social distinction
    88; struggles 35
classic sociological structure *vs.*
    agency 88
Click, Melissa 68
CNN 15
The Colour Purple film 66
commercial culture 43
commercial television (ITV) 51n5
communication 13, 70, 108
The Communist Manifesto (Marx and
    Engels) 36
'composite' environment 25
compulsory individuality 124
conduct audience analysis 98
confidence culture 20
conjunctural analysis 24–26, 25, 156,
    157–161; consumption 158–159; form
    158; identity 160–161; production
    158; regulation 159; representation
    159–160
conjunctural critique 2, 156–157
conjuncture 7, 26–27, 59, 71, 87, 106,
    142, 149
consumer behaviour 98
contagion 106–109
contemporary civic actions 17
contemporary media 4, 11, 43, 44,
    59, 150
content creators 126, 143, 145
convergence culture 14, 89
Corner, John 72, 74
corporate fitness 159
The Cosby Show 66
cosmopolitan sensitivities 76

INDEX **167**

Couldry, Nick 13, 23, 149, 150
Covid pandemic 1, 158–159
Craig, D. 120, 130, 143
creator culture 143
The Creator Union 118–119
critical ability 41
critical audience studies 66–68
cultural capital 87–88, 92, 99
cultural circuit 23, 24, 64, 142, 149–151, 154, 156, 157
Cultural Studies model 22, 59, 62, 141; active audience 63–66; audience, notion of 136; audience research 4; circuit of culture 23
culture/cultural 95; affective turn 96; context 17; dopes 69; feelings of 86; geography 97; industry 36; life 13; power 64
Cunningham, S. 76, 120, 130, 143
Curran, J. 16

Dahlgren, Peter 146
Dalgren, Peter 142
Dallas 94
Das, Ranjana 26, 69, 149
data: activism 23; algorithms 24; audiences 20; colonialism 22; justice 23; surveillance 2
datafication 13, 23, 142, 150
Davis, Aeron 43
Dean, Jodi 107
De Beneditis, S. 106
De Certeau, Michel 91
deconstructivism 97
De Kosnik, Abigail 126
Deleuze, Gilles 97, 99, 106
Denisova, A. 145
Dependant, Distracted, Bored (Paasonen) 86
detextualisation 44
'de-westernise' media studies 32
Dialectic of Enlightenment (Adorno and Horkheimer) 36
Dickens, L. 23
digi-gratis economy 93

digital: diaspora 17; economy 11, 125, 126, 134; elite 134; environment 4, 14, 25, 26, 74, 142, 146, 155; landscape 125, 128; media audiences 17; natives generation 18, 45; sphere 94; *see also individual entries*
digital age 6, 31, 85; audiencing 68, 141; techno-social formations 143
digital circuit 136, 150–156, 155; audience sensitive approach 141; cultural processes 142
digital culture 8, 86, 152; affective formations 86; character of 15; cultural studies 141; engagements with 145; fast-paced dynamism 156; meaning-making 152; social interaction 61
Digital Fandom 69
digitalisation 17
digital labour 129, 133, 134
Digital Labour (Jarrett) 133
dispersed audiences 2
Distinction: A Social Critique of the Judgement of Taste (Bourdieu) 87
Divination 33
Doing Cultural Studies (Du Gay and Madsen) 150, 151
domestic audience 41
Dosekun, Simidele 20
Doty, Alexander 67
Douglas, Susan 47
Dourish, Paul 22
Dovey, Jon 124
Duffy, B.E. 129
Du Gay, Paul 7, 149, 151

economic business models 11
economistic model 121
effects 22, 40, 41, 43–44, 50, 60
emotion/emotional 97; analysis 86; engagements 23; feminist audience research 93–94; labour 134; psychoanalytic dimensions of 95; realism 87, 90–93, 94
'encoding and decoding' model 64, 65

168 INDEX

engagement: audience engagements 11; emotional engagements 23; media engagements 15
Engels, F. 36
Enlightenment project 36
entertainment media 19
entrepreneurialism 19, 133
environmental crisis 2
essentialism 156
ethnographic sensibility 74–77, 76
ethnography 37, 74
Eubanks, Virginia 24
European tradition 35
Evanss, Elizabeth 15, 61
exploitation 130–133
extension audiences 17

Facebook 107, 128, 132, 154
faltering democracy 2
Family Television 74
fan: communities 93; cultures 90–93; labour 126–127; management strategies 93
Fan Cultures (Hills) 92
fascism 33
Feasey, Rebecca 68
feel/feeling: audience engagements 85; individual feelings 95; media audiences 85–87; quantification of 107; social relations 85–87; structure of 85–87, 94, 108; taste and value 87
feminised sphere 133–135
feminist audience work 37, 93
Feminist Media Studies 68
feminist project 38, 46
feminist reception studies 68
Fenton, N. 16
Fifty Shades of Grey 68
file-sharing 16
film censorship 40
finstas (Fake Instagram accounts) 1
Fisher, Eran 128
Fiske, John 5, 24, 68, 90, 91
Floating Lives (Sinclair and Cunningham) 76

Flow (Jenkins) 90
Forest Hill group 111n7
form 24, 158
Fotopoulou, A. 23
Foucault, Michel 96
Frankfurt school 18, 35, 59, 60, 120, 121
Fraser, Nancy 94
free labour 22, 122, 124–126, 130, 131
Freeman, D. 16
Fuchs, C. 108

gaming approach 148
gender orders 2
The Generic Closet (Martin) 67
Giddens, Anthony 73, 124
gift-economy 126
gig economy 18
Gillespie, Marie 75, 77
Gill, Ros 19, 20
Gilroy, Paul 96
Goggin, Joyce 126
Gogglebox (television programme) 56–58, 62, 73
Google 21, 154
Google Play 159
Gorton, Kristyn 98
Govil, Nitin 144
Gramscian-influenced critical position 59, 63
Gramsci, Antonio 63, 86
gratifications model 64–65
Gray, Ann 4, 75
Gray, Jonathan 26, 89
Gregg, Melissa 21
Grossberg, Lawrence 66, 100
Gunning, Tom 39
Gurevitch, M. 71

Habermas, Jurgen 94
Hall, Stuart 64, 149, 150
Hancock, B.H. 91
Harrington, C. Lee 91, 107
Harrisson, Tom 48
Harvey, David 127
Hay, J. 124

INDEX 169

Hearn, Alison 127
Helmond, A. 154
Hemming, Claire 97
Hepp, Andrea 13
Hermes, Joke 75
Hesmondhalgh, David 131
heteronormative audiences 67
Hill, Annette 124, 142, 146
Hills, Matt 92
historical audience 44–49
Hobson, Dorothy 37, 68, 75
homophobia 90
'hook-up' culture 68
Horkheimer, Max 35, 36, 121
Horton, D. 42
housewife aged 18 30–31, 49
hypercomplexity 11
hypodermic syringe model 43

ideological ethos 120
imagined audience 144
immaterial labour 129, 133
impression management 144
individualism 26, 63
individual self-love 10
industrial capitalism 119
industrialisation 34–35, 39
influencers 18, 129–130; digital
   economy 134; female influencers 130;
   inequalities 133–135; public relations
   42; social media 120; YouTube,
   middle-class influencers 134
Instagram 10, 129, 154; image-led
   platform 129; micro-celebrity 14
internet 2, 15, 70, 133; advertising
   revenue 123; characteristic of
   34; digital audiences 69; digital
   poorhouse 24; of dreams 16; users
   61, 70
interpersonal relationships 11
interpretation 63–64
intimate public sphere 110

Jansson, A. 76
Jarrett, Kylie 133

Jenkins, Henry 90, 91
Jenkins, Rather 91
Jennings, Humphrey 48
Jhally, Sut 66, 122
Johnson, Richard 150, 152
juvenile behaviour 40

Katz, E. 71
Kay, Jilly 100
Kember, Sarah 143
Kennedy, Helen 23
Kennedy, Melanie 100
Khalil, Joe F. 36
Kim, Youna 67
K-Pop phenomena 90
#KpopTwitter 84–85
Krüger, S. 148
Kuhn, Annette 40, 46

labour: affect/affective 111, 127; of
   authenticity 130; digital labour 129,
   133, 134; emotion/emotional 134;
   fan labour 126–127; free labour 22;
   immaterial labour 129; labour theory
   128; Marxist distinction 121; platform
   labour 134; queer labour 127; tacit
   labour 130; visibility labour 130; wage
   labour 35
Ladies Peloton Facebook group 10
Lazarsfeld, P. 42
Le Bon, G. 33
left-ish quasi-political social movement
   51n4
'legacy' media 2, 11
Lewis, Justin 66
LGBTQ+: audiences 98; fandom 93
Life on the Screen (Turkle) 47
lifestyle media 124
Limperos, A. 62
linguistic interpretative frame 72
Livant, B. 122
lived cultures 4
Livingstone, Sonia 23, 26, 32, 43, 44,
   69, 149
London Stock Exchange 44

INDEX

loneliness 86
Longhurst, Brian 2
The Long Revolution (Williams) 86
Lull, James 75
Lunenborg, M. 103

machine-algorithms 132, 135
macro and micro audience model 16
Madge, Charles 48
Madianou, Mirca 76
Magaluf Girl 98
magic bullet theory 40
Maier, T. 103
mainstream media 16
Make Room for TV (Spigel) 48
Mankekar, Purnima 37, 75, 94
Martin, Alfred 67
Martschukat, Jürgen 159
Marwick, A. E. 134, 144
Marx, Karl 35, 36
mass audience 35, 36, 41, 43
mass communications 15, 35, 61
mass dopes 91
mass media 32, 34, 39
mass mediated communication 62
Mass Observation Archives 45, 48, 51n1
mass persuasion 42
mass self-communication 61
mass society 37
Massumi, Brian 96–97
McQuail, Denis 61, 71, 75
meaning-making practices 59–60, 71,
  97; active audience 63–66; uses and
  gratifications 60–63
media: audiences 1, 18, 47, 59,
  85–87; behaviourist models of 65;
  complexity 18; consumption 6, 60,
  65; educational appeal 71; egalitarian
  model of 16; engagements 15, 25;
  environment 3; ethnographies
  76; positivistic approaches 24;
  production 14; profit-making
  strategies 126; technologies 32;
  transitional objects 92
Media and Cultural Studies approach 2, 5

media landscape 12, 61;
  democratisation of 11;
  transmediality 15
media logic 13
Media Matters (Hancock) 91
media ownership 15, 90
mediated conversational floor 73
media texts 15, 68
media theory 98
mediatisation 12–13, 23, 60, 149
Meehan, Eileen 122, 132
Mejias, U. 23
melodramatic imagination 94, 110
memory 44–49
Merton, P. 42
Merton, R. 42
#MeToo moment 16, 107
Mhabharat 75
micro-activism 144
micro-celebrity 14, 128–129, 144
migrant populations 76
misinformation 41
mobile media 17
mobile vulgus 34
modality 16
monopoly capitalism 121
Moores, Shaun 76
moral judgement 102
Morley, David 42, 65, 74, 75, 102, 150
Movies and Conduct (Blumer) 40
multi-mediated audience 69
Mutlu, B. 90

Nafus, Dawn 21
nationalism 90
Nationwide (television programme) 65
The Nationwide Audience (Morley) 150
Nelson, J.L. 41
neoliberal culture 100, 103
neoliberal ideologies 19–20
neoliberalism 20, 105, 146
networked media 32
network effects 21
New Addington group 111n7
new media studies 70

INDEX **171**

Noble, Safiya 24, 134
'non-media centric' media studies 77
non-representational theory 97
normativity 99
North Atlantic modernity 13

Occupy movement 107
Ofcom 1
'omnivorous' tastes 88
One Born Every Minute 106
online: audience activity 21, 37;
    audience behaviour 41; configuration
    149; digital platforms 14;
    environment 94
online-offline experiences 38
Orcran, Nicola 118
Orgad, S. 20
Osseiran, S. 77
Ouellette, L. 124

Paasonen, Susannah 86
Papacharizzi, Zizi 17, 107
Parables for the Virtual (Massumi) 96
para-social interaction 42, 73, 129
para-social relationships 26, 158
participation paradigm 69
participatory culture 16, 69, 108
passive audience model 16
Peloton fitness bike 9–10, 15, 157–161
Peloton Interactive Inc. 158
Penny Gaffs 39
'people-focussed' approach 23
performers 122
periodisation approach 13
personal realm 94
Petley, J. 44
platforms 1, 18, 21, 23, 24, 62, 107;
    capitalism 37; labour 134; media 32
podcasting 16
pointless populism 69
political economy 7, 90, 120, 121
political power 64
political structure 95
polymedia 25, 76
popular cultural capital 69, 92

popular entertainment 34
populism 33
post-audience age 68
post-colonial landscape 96
postfeminism 20
post-Fordist capitalism 127
post-imperial melancholia 96
post-war housing projects 49
Press, Andrea 68
Privacy Policy 159
Probyn, E. 103
producer 15
produsage 2, 15, 17
produsers 13
profit-making strategies 126
pseudo-relationships 42
psychoanalytical frameworks 92
public space 37
Pygmalion narratives 101

quasi-operating systems 153
queer audience research 67
queer labour 127

racial capitalism 2
radio 39, 40; archaeology of 47
Radway, Janice 37
Reacting to Reality Television (Skeggs
    and Wood) 101
'real' audiences 22
reality television 87, 100–106, 125
reductionism 156
reflexive sociology 76
resilience: neoliberal ideologies of 20
revisionism 33, 42, 44–49
revolutionised fandom 69
Ripat, Pauline 33
Rosa, Harmut 19

Sandvoss, Gray 91
Scandal (ABC TV series) 108
Scannell, Paddy 35, 42, 72
Seigworth, Greg 106
self-branding 127–129
self-optimisation 145

172 INDEX

self-performance 123
self-reliance, neoliberal ideologies 20
self-transformation 101
self-work, neoliberal ideologies 20
Sender, Katherine 68
sensitivity 76
sexuality, politics of 68
sexual violence 16
shadowy popular majority 33
Sharma, Sarah 19
Shaw, Adrienne 68
Sherlock (BBC television series) 127
Shome, Raka 13
Silverstone, Roger 62
Simon, Victoria 147
Sinclair, J. 76
Skeggs, Beverley 99, 103, 132
Slack, J.D. 156
slacktivism 145
Smythe, Dallas 121, 122, 125
Snow, R.P. 13
sociability 62
social: acceleration 19; concerns 37; contexts 49, 71, 72, 95; determinism 97; domination 100; formation 25; inequality 2; landscape 91; processes 12; psychologists 107; realm 100–106; relationships 74, 85–87; sciences 86
social change 3, 44, 47; audience histories 31–33; media's relationship with 31, 43
social life 13, 35, 71
social media 1, 12, 15, 17, 18, 21, 37, 42, 107, 120, 123, 125; audience 106–109; connectivity of 86; entertainment industry 143; as free labour 126; influencers 18; power of 107; relationships 43
social networking sites (SNS) 41
socio-economic reality 66
socio-historical junctures 32
socio-political conjuncture 101
socio-political context 17
socio-political formation 78
socio-technological environment 154

spectacular subjectivity 124
spectatorship 8
Spigel, Lynn 48, 49
Spilde, A. 148
Srnicke, Nick 21
Stacey, Jackie 45
Stanfill, Mel 93, 126, 147
Star Gazing (Stacey) 45
Star Trek fans 69, 130
storycircle project 23
Strathern, Marilyn 124
Striphas, Ted 153
structural political formations 76
structure of feeling 86, 94, 98, 108; definition 108
students watching television 25
sub-cultural capital 92
subjectivity 73, 92
Suffrage movement 39
Sunder, S. 62
surveillance capitalism 22
symbolic annihilation 134
symbolic warfare 90
Syrian and Iraqi refugees 77

tacit labour 130
Talking With Television 62, 72, 78
Taneja, H. 41
Tarde, Gabriel 107
taste, economistic model of 87
Taylor, Charles 124
techno-determinist approach 17
technological change 3, 19, 32
technological insurgency 47
techno-social arrangements 2
techno-social change 12
television 48, 152; audiences 15, 121; social uses of 75
Terranova, Titziana 125
testing ambiguities 99–100
text–reader relationship 72
textuality 73
textual poachers 91
#Thisisacoup 107
Thompson, John 12

INDEX **173**

Thrift, Nigel 97
Thumim, Janet 48
TikTok 1, 38, 49, 126, 128, 133, 154
time-management systems 19
top-down ideological power 91
traditional media 15
transitional objects 92
transmediality 15
transmission 16
'trapping' women 66
Trump, Donald 108
Tufte, Thomas 75
Turkle, Sherry 18, 47
TV talk shows 89
Twitter 14, 15, 107, 108, 109, 144
Twitter Revolutions 16
Tyler, Imogen 98
typology 61

urban poverty 35
US communications theory 59
user-generated content 16
users 11, 16, 21, 128–129, 158
'uses and gratifications' model 59–63

value struggle 106
van Dijck, J. 149
The Velveteen Rabbit (Jenkins) 91
video-sharing 16
visibility labour 130

wage labour 35
warm bodies, audiences 12, 22–24, 141, 148
War of the Worlds, HG Wells 41
Wetherall, Margie 95, 98
Whatsapp 154
Wife Swap (TV programme) 103
wikis 16
Willems, Wendy 20
Williams, Raymond 3, 4, 86, 95, 106, 108, 110, 157
Wohl, R. 42
women: confidence culture 20; consumer freedoms 37; emotional labour 95; television, reflexive relationships 67
workers, audiences 17–19
working-class tastes 88
World Wide Web 153
Wright, Erik Olin 131

youth audiences 45
YouTube 14, 15, 62, 71, 120, 123, 128, 133, 154
Ytre-Arne, Brit 26, 149
Yuill, Simon 132

zero-sum game 18
Zylinska, Joanna 143

Printed in the United States
by Baker & Taylor Publisher Services